Q: Skills for Success

READING AND WRITING

3

Teacher's Handbook

Jenni Currie Santamaria

OXFORD
UNIVERSITY PRESS

OXFORD
UNIVERSITY PRESS

198 Madison Avenue
New York, NY 10016 USA

Great Clarendon Street, Oxford OX2 6DP UK

Oxford University Press is a department of the University of Oxford.
It furthers the University's objective of excellence in research, scholarship,
and education by publishing worldwide in

Oxford New York

Auckland Cape Town Dar es Salaam Hong Kong Karachi
Kuala Lumpur Madrid Melbourne Mexico City Nairobi
New Delhi Shanghai Taipei Toronto

With offices in

Argentina Austria Brazil Chile Czech Republic France Greece
Guatemala Hungary Italy Japan Poland Portugal Singapore
South Korea Switzerland Thailand Turkey Ukraine Vietnam

OXFORD and OXFORD ENGLISH are registered trademarks of
Oxford University Press.

General Manager, American ELT: Laura Pearson
Publisher: Stephanie Karras
Associate Publishing Manager: Sharon Sargent
Associate Development Editor: Keyana Shaw
Director, ADP: Susan Sanguily
Executive Design Manager: Maj-Britt Hagsted
Associate Design Manager: Michael Steinhofer
Electronic Production Manager: Julie Armstrong
Production Artist: Elissa Santos
Cover Design: Michael Steinhofer
Production Coordinator: Elizabeth Matsumoto

ISBN: 978-0-19-475629-7 Reading and Writing 3 Teacher's Handbook Pack
ISBN: 978-0-19-475654-9 Reading and Writing 3 Teacher's Handbook
ISBN: 978-0-19-475669-3 Reading & Writing/Listening & Speaking 3
 Testing Program CD-ROM
ISBN: 978-0-19-475643-3 Q Online Practice Teacher Access Code Card

Printed in China

This book is printed on paper from certified and well-managed sources.

10 9 8 7 6 5 4 3 2

ACKNOWLEDGMENTS

*The publishers would like to thank the following for their kind permission to reproduce
photographs:*
p. vi Marcin Krygier/iStockphoto; xiii Rüstem GÜRLER/iStockphoto

CONTENTS

Welcome to *Q*   iv

To the Teacher   v

Student Book Quick Guide   viii

Student Book Scope and Sequence   xiv

Unit 1   Q: How do you make a good first impression?
    Teaching Notes   2
    Unit Assignment Rubric   12

Unit 2   Q: What makes food taste good?
    Teaching Notes   13
    Unit Assignment Rubric   22

Unit 3   Q: What does it take to be successful?
    Teaching Notes   23
    Unit Assignment Rubric   33

Unit 4   Q: How has technology affected your life?
    Teaching Notes   34
    Unit Assignment Rubric   44

Unit 5   Q: Why do people help each other?
    Teaching Notes   45
    Unit Assignment Rubric   55

Unit 6   Q: Does advertising help or harm us?
    Teaching Notes   56
    Unit Assignment Rubric   65

Unit 7   Q: Why do people take risks?
    Teaching Notes   66
    Unit Assignment Rubric   75

Unit 8   Q: How can we make cities better places to live?
    Teaching Notes   76
    Unit Assignment Rubric   86

Unit 9   Q: How can a small amount of money make a big difference?
    Teaching Notes   87
    Unit Assignment Rubric   97

Unit 10   Q: Do people communicate better now than in the past?
    Teaching Notes   98
    Unit Assignment Rubric   108

How to use the *Q* Testing Program CD-ROM   109

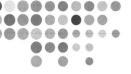

WELCOME TO **Q**:Skills for Success

Q: Skills for Success is a six-level series with two strands,
Reading and Writing **and** *Listening and Speaking.*

WITH Q ONLINE PRACTICE web

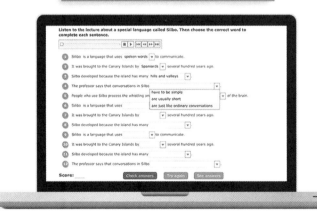

STUDENT AND TEACHER INFORMED

Q: Skills for Success is the result of an extensive development process involving thousands of teachers and hundreds of students around the world. Their views and opinions helped shape the content of the series. *Q* is grounded in teaching theory as well as real-world classroom practice, making it the most learner-centered series available.

To the Teacher

Highlights of the *Q: Skills for Success* Teacher's Handbook

As you probably know from your own teaching experience, students want to know the point of a lesson. They want to know the "why" even when they understand the "how." In the classroom, the "why" is the learning outcome, and to be successful, students need to know it. The learning outcome provides a clear reason for classroom work and helps students meaningfully access new material.

Each unit in Oxford's *Q: Skills for Success* series builds around a thought-provoking question related to that unit's unique learning outcome. Students learn vocabulary to answer the unit question; consider new information related to the unit's theme that utilizes this vocabulary; use this information to think critically about new questions; and use those answers to practice the new reading, vocabulary, grammar, and writing skills they need to achieve the unit's learning outcome.

Each aspect of the learning process in the Q series builds toward completing the learning outcome. This interconnected process of considering new information is at the heart of a critical thinking approach and forms the basis of the students' work in each unit of the Q series. At the end of the unit, students complete a practical project built around the learning outcome.

Learning outcomes create expectations in the classroom: expectations of what students will learn, what teachers will teach, and what lessons will focus on. Students benefit because they know they need to learn content for a purpose; teachers benefit because they can plan activities that reinforce the knowledge and skills students need to complete the learning outcome. In short, learning outcomes provide the focus that lessons need.

In this example unit, students are asked to think about and discuss what makes them laugh.

The unit assignment ties into that unit's unique learning outcome.

UNIT **6**

Unit QUESTION
What makes you laugh?

Laughter

READING • identifying the topic sentence in a paragraph
VOCABULARY • using the dictionary
GRAMMAR • sentences with *when*
WRITING • writing a topic sentence

LEARNING OUTCOME
Explain what makes you or someone you know laugh.

Writing a Paragraph	20 points	15 points	10 points	0 points
The first line of the paragraph is indented, and the paragraph has an appropriate topic sentence.				
Sentences with *when* and *because* are correct.				
Paragraph explains what makes someone laugh using vocabulary from the unit.				
Sentences begin with capital letters and end with appropriate punctuation.				
Every sentence has a subject and a verb and they are in agreement.				

Total points: _____
Comments:

Clear assessments allow both teachers and students to comment on and measure learner outcomes.

► *Reading and Writing 1, page 116*

Unit Assignment: Write a paragraph about what makes someone laugh

Unit Question (5 minutes)

Refer students back to the ideas they discussed at the beginning of the unit about laughter. Ask: *What makes you or someone you know laugh?* Bring out the answers students wrote on poster paper at the beginning of the unit. Cue students if necessary by asking specific questions about the content of the unit: *Why is laughter important? What makes you laugh the hardest? What kinds of things do you find funny? What kinds of things are not funny?* Read the direction lines for the assignment together to ensure understanding.

Learning Outcome

1. Tie the Unit Assignment to the unit learning outcome. Say: *The outcome for this unit is to explain what makes you or someone you know laugh. This Unit Assignment is going to let you show your skill at writing paragraphs, using a topic sentence, and writing sentences with* when *and* because.

CRITICAL THINKING

A critical thinking approach asks students to process new information and to learn how to apply that information to a new situation. Teachers might set learning outcomes to give students targets to hit—for example: "After this lesson, give three reasons why people immigrate"—and the materials and exercises in the lesson provide students with the knowledge and skills to think critically and discover *their* three reasons.

Questions are important catalysts in the critical thinking process. Questions encourage students to reflect on and apply their knowledge to new situations. Students and teachers work together to understand, analyze, synthesize, and evaluate the lesson's questions and content to reach the stated outcomes. As students become more familiar with these stages of the critical thinking process, they will be able to use new information to complete tasks more efficiently and in unique and meaningful ways.

Tip Critical Thinking

In Activity B, you have to **restate**, or say again in perhaps a different way, some of the information you learned in the two readings. **Restating** is a good way to review information.

Throughout the Student Book, *Critical Thinking Tips* accompany certain activities, helping students to practice and understand these critical thinking skills.

B (10 minutes)

1. Introduce the Unit Question, *Why do people immigrate to other countries?* Ask related information questions or questions about personal experience to help students prepare for answering the more abstract unit question: *Did you immigrate to this country? What were your reasons for leaving your home country? What were your reasons for choosing your new country? What did you bring with you?*

2. Tell students: *Let's start off our discussion by listing reasons why people might immigrate. For example, we could start our list with* finding work *because many people look for jobs in new countries. But there are many other reasons why people immigrate. What else can we think of?*

Critical Thinking Tip (1 minute)

1. Read the tip aloud.
2. Tell students that restating also helps to ensure that they have understood something correctly. After reading a new piece of information, they should try to restate it to a classmate who has also read the information, to ensure that they both have the same understanding of information.

The *Q Teacher's Handbook* features notes offering questions for expanded thought and discussion.

CRITICAL Q EXPANSION ACTIVITIES

The *Q Teacher's Handbook* expands on the critical thinking approach with the Critical Q Expansion Activities. These activities allow teachers to facilitate more practice for their students. The Critical Q Expansion Activities supplement the *Q Student Book* by expanding on skills and language students are practicing.

In today's classrooms, it's necessary that students have the ability to apply the skills they have learned to new situations with materials they have never seen before. Q's focus on critical thinking and the *Q Teacher's Handbook's* emphasis on practicing critical thinking skills through the Critical Q Expansion Activities prepares students to excel in this important skill.

Critical Q: Expansion Activity

Outlining

1. Explain to students: *A popular way to prepare to outline one's ideas is to use a cluster map. In a cluster map, a big circle is drawn in the middle of a page or on the board, and a main point is written inside it—**this will become the topic sentence in the outline.***

2. Then explain: *Next, lines are drawn away from the circle and new, smaller circles are attached to the other end of those lines. Inside each of the smaller circles, ideas are written which relate to the main point—**these become supporting sentences in the outline.***

The easy-to-use activity suggestions increase student practice and success with critical thinking skills.

21ST CENTURY SKILLS

Both the academic and professional worlds are becoming increasingly interdependent. The toughest problems are solved only when looked at from multiple perspectives. Success in the 21st century requires more than just core academic knowledge—though that is still crucial. Now, successful students have to collaborate, innovate, adapt, be self-directed, be flexible, be creative, be tech-literate, practice teamwork, and be accountable—both individually and in groups.

Q approaches language learning in light of these important 21st Century Skills. Each unit asks students to practice many of these attributes, from collaboration to innovation to accountability, *while* they are learning new language and content. The Q *Student Books* focus on these increasingly important skills with unique team, pair, and individual activities. Additionally, the Q *Teacher's Handbooks* provide support with easy-to-use 21st Century Skill sections for teachers who want to incorporate skills like "openness to other people's ideas and opinions" into their classrooms but aren't sure where to start.

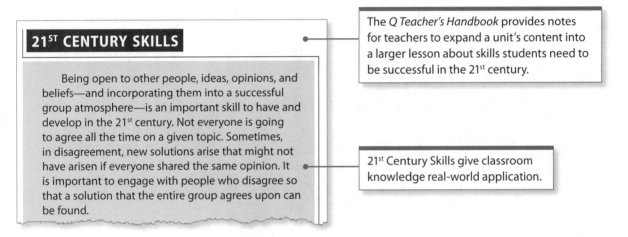

21ST CENTURY SKILLS

Being open to other people, ideas, opinions, and beliefs—and incorporating them into a successful group atmosphere—is an important skill to have and develop in the 21st century. Not everyone is going to agree all the time on a given topic. Sometimes, in disagreement, new solutions arise that might not have arisen if everyone shared the same opinion. It is important to engage with people who disagree so that a solution that the entire group agrees upon can be found.

The Q *Teacher's Handbook* provides notes for teachers to expand a unit's content into a larger lesson about skills students need to be successful in the 21st century.

21st Century Skills give classroom knowledge real-world application.

Q ONLINE PRACTICE

Q *Online Practice* is an online workbook that gives students quick access to all-new content in a range of additional practice activities. The interface is intuitive and user-friendly, allowing students to focus on enhancing their language skills.

For the teacher, Q *Online Practice* includes a digital grade book providing immediate and accurate assessment of each student's progress. Straightforward individual student or class reports can be viewed onscreen, printed, or exported, giving you comprehensive feedback on what students have mastered or where they need more help.

Teacher's Access Code Cards for the digital grade book are available upon adoption or for purchase. Use the access code to register for your Q *Online Practice* account at www.Qonlinepractice.com.

These features of the Q: *Skills for Success* series enable you to help your students develop the skills they need to succeed in their future academic and professional careers. By using learning outcomes, critical thinking, and 21st century skills, you help students gain a deeper knowledge of the material they are presented with, both in and out of the classroom.

Q connects critical thinking, language skills, and learning outcomes.

LANGUAGE SKILLS

Explicit skills instruction enables students to meet their academic and professional goals.

LEARNING OUTCOMES

Clearly identified **learning outcomes** focus students on the goal of their instruction.

UNIT **5**

Responsibility

READING ● using a graphic organizer
VOCABULARY ● phrasal verbs
WRITING ● stating reasons and giving examples
GRAMMAR ● gerunds and infinitives

LEARNING OUTCOME

Write a paragraph about why people help others using reasons and examples.

Unit QUESTION

Why do people help each other?

PREVIEW THE UNIT

A Discuss these questions with your classmates.

Did your parents teach you to be helpful to others? Is being helpful something we learn, or is it human nature?

Are there any situations in which you don't think you should help someone? Explain.

Look at the photo. What do you think is happening?

B Discuss the Unit Question above with your classmates.

Listen to *The Q Classroom*, Track 2 on CD 2, **to hear other answers.**

88 UNIT 5

89

CRITICAL THINKING

Thought-provoking **unit questions** engage students with the topic and provide a **critical thinking framework** for the unit.

 Having the learning outcome is important because it gives students and teachers a clear idea of what the point of each task/activity in the unit is.
Lawrence Lawson, Palomar College, California

The Biology of Altruism

1 Scientific evidence suggests that humans have a biological desire to help others, including strangers. **Altruistic** behavior towards strangers is uniquely human and observed at a very young age. Dr. Felix Warneken and Dr. Michael Tomasello of Germany's Max Planck Institute for Evolutionary Anthropology have shown that children as young as 18 months want to help strangers. When their 18-month-old **subjects** saw a stranger throw a pencil on the floor, none of them picked it up. However, when the same subjects saw someone "accidentally" drop a pencil, nearly all the children picked it up in the first ten seconds. Says Dr. Warneken, "The results were astonishing because these children are so young. They still wear diapers and are **barely** able to use language, but they already show helping behavior." Because altruistic behavior appears in children so young, Dr. Warneken and other scientists **hypothesize** that the human brain is designed to be altruistic.

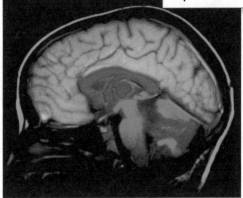

Brain scans like this one help scientists see the brain in action.

cry or smile when someone smiles at us. Our mirror neurons actually feel what they feel. They cry and smile along with them.

3 How, then, can mirror neurons **bring about** altruistic behavior? By helping us feel what others feel, mirror neurons naturally make us feel **compassionate**. They allow us to put ourselves in someone else's situation; without them, we would not understand or

 **WHAT DO YOU THINK?**

A. Discuss the questions in a group.

1. How altruistic do you think you are? Give examples to support your opinion.

2. Why do you think some people are more altruistic than others?

 One of the best features is your focus on developing materials of a high "interest level."
Troy Hammond, Tokyo Gakugei University, International Secondary School, Japan

Explicit skills instruction prepares students for academic success.

LANGUAGE SKILLS

Explicit instruction and practice in reading, vocabulary, grammar, and writing skills **help students achieve language proficiency.**

LEARNING OUTCOMES

Practice activities allow students to **master the skills** before they are evaluated at the end of the unit.

Q² WHAT DO YOU THINK?

Discuss the questions in a group. Then choose one question and write five to eight sentences in response.

1. Have you ever *not* helped someone who needed help? Why or why not? What factors might make someone choose not to help a stranger?

2. In general, which people do you think are more helpful to strangers in need: people who live in cities or people who live in small towns? Why?

3. The author of "A Question of Numbers" writes that "some cultures might put more importance on helping strangers than others do." Do you think that a person's culture can be a factor in making him or her a more helpful person? Why or why not?

Reading Skill | Using a graphic organizer

Graphic organizers represent ideas with images, such as diagrams, charts, tables, and timelines. You can use graphic organizers to help you see connections between ideas or remember the main points of a text or parts of a text. Using graphic organizers can help you review a text you have read in preparation for class or a test.

The flowchart below organizes the main points of a scientific article.

WRITING

Writing Skill | Using descriptive adjectives

Adjectives are words that describe nouns (*people, places, things,* and *ideas*). Writers use a lot of adjectives in order to make their descriptions both interesting and clear. They describe what they *see, hear, smell, taste, touch,* and *feel.* They paint a picture with words so that readers can easily imagine or "see" what they are describing. Using **descriptive adjectives** in your writing will make it more interesting for the reader.

Non-descriptive: I ate a meal at a restaurant downtown.
Descriptive: I ate a **delicious, savory** meal at a **cozy French** restaurant downtown.

A. Read the paragraph. Then answer the questions with a partner.

My Mother's Yorkshire Pudding

Whenever I think of my mother's cooking, I always remember her delicious Yorkshire puddings. Although I grew up in the United States, my mother often cooked dishes from her home country of England. She has always been an excellent cook, and one of her best recipes is called Yorkshire pudding, which is a traditional English pastry. It is a simple dish made with eggs, flour, and milk. My mother's Yorkshire puddings taste so good because they are light, crisp, and slightly sweet. She serves them with delicious warm gravy, but I prefer them sweet with strawberry jam. They are very special because she only serves them on holidays. My sister and I always fight for the last one because they are so delicious. I have had many other people's Yorkshire puddings, but my mother's have always tasted better. Not only are hers homemade, but they also have a special taste that always makes me think of her. They also make me remember my British ancestry and my mother's history. They help me connect to my past and to my family. Yorkshire pudding is such a simple and common English food, but it will always be special to me because of my mother.

1. What is the topic sentence? Underline it.
2. What is the concluding sentence? Underline it.
3. How does Yorkshire pudding taste? Circle the sentence that describes the taste.

 The tasks are simple, accessible, user-friendly, and very useful.
Jessica March, American University of Sharjah, U.A.E.

Q Online Practice provides all new content for additional practice in an easy-to-use online workbook. Every student book includes a *Q Online Practice access code card*. Use the access code to register for your *Q Online Practice* account at www.Qonlinepractice.com.

Vocabulary Skill | **Using the dictionary**

Word Forms

Learning word forms increases your vocabulary. It will help make your reading, speaking, and writing more fluent. Look at the dictionary definitions below.

ac·com·plish /əˈkɑmplɪʃ/ *verb* [T] to succeed in doing something difficult that you planned to do: *Very little was accomplished at the meeting.* **SYN achieve**

ac·com·plished /əˈkɑmplɪʃt/ *adj.* highly skilled at something: *an accomplished pianist*

ac·com·plish·ment /əˈkɑmplɪʃmənt/ *noun* **1** [C] something difficult that someone has succeeded in doing or learning: *He was proud of his academic accomplishments.* **2** (*formal*) [U] the act of completing something successfully

All dictionary entries are taken from the *Oxford American Dictionary for learners of English*.

LANGUAGE SKILLS

A **research-based vocabulary program** focuses students on the words they need to know academically and professionally, using skill strategies based on the same research as the Oxford dictionaries.

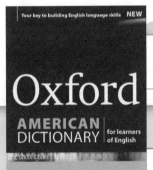

All dictionary entries are taken from the *Oxford American Dictionary for learners of English*.

The *Oxford American Dictionary for learners of English* was developed with English learners in mind, and provides extra learning tools for pronunciation, verb types, basic grammar structures, and more.

The Oxford 3000™ 🔑
The Oxford 3000 encompasses **the 3000 most important words to learn in English.** It is based on a comprehensive analysis of the Oxford English Corpus, a two-billion word collection of English text, and on extensive research with both language and pedagogical experts.

The Academic Word List **AWL**
The Academic Word List was created by Averil Coxhead and contains **570 words that are commonly used in academic English,** such as in textbooks or articles across a wide range of academic subject areas. These words are a great place to start if you are studying English for academic purposes.

Clear learning outcomes focus students on the goals of instruction.

LEARNING OUTCOMES

A culminating unit assignment evaluates the students' **mastery of the learning outcome.**

Unit Assignment | Write a paragraph with reasons and examples

 In this assignment, you are going to write a paragraph with reasons and examples. As you prepare your paragraph, think about the Unit Question, "Why do people help each other?" Refer to the Self-Assessment checklist on page 110. Use information from Readings 1 and 2 and your work in this unit to support your ideas.

For alternative unit assignments, see the *Q: Skills for Success Teacher's Handbook*.

PLAN AND WRITE

A. **BRAINSTORM** In a group, brainstorm reasons other than than the ones in the readings that might affect a person's decision to help others. Write your ideas in your notebook.

B. **PLAN** Follow these steps as you plan your paragraph.

1. Look at your notes from Activity A. Circle the reasons you want to include in your paragraph. Then think of examples to support these reasons.

2. Think about the readings in this unit. Is there any information from them that can help support your ideas?

LEARNER CENTERED

Track Your Success allows students to **assess their own progress** and provides guidance on remediation.

Check (✓) the skills you learned. If you need more work on a skill, refer to the page(s) in parentheses.

READING	● I can use a graphic organizer. (p. 96)
VOCABULARY	● I can use phrasal verbs. (p. 103)
WRITING	● I can state reasons and give examples. (p. 105)
GRAMMAR	● I can use gerunds and infinitives. (p. 107)
LEARNING OUTCOME	● I can write a paragraph about why people help others using reasons and examples.

 Students can check their learning ... and they can focus on the essential points when they study.

Suh Yoomi, Seoul, South Korea

Q Online Practice

For the student

- **Easy-to-use:** a simple interface allows students to focus on enhancing their speaking and listening skills, not learning a new software program
- **Flexible:** for use anywhere there's an Internet connection
- **Access code card:** a *Q Online Practice* access code is included with the student book. Use the access code to register for *Q Online Practice* at www.Qonlinepractice.com

For the teacher

- **Simple yet powerful:** automatically grades student exercises and tracks progress
- **Straightforward:** online management system to review, print, or export reports
- **Flexible:** for use in the classroom or easily assigned as homework
- **Access code card:** contact your sales rep for your *Q Online Practice* teacher's access code

Teacher Resources

Oxford **Teachers' Club**

For additional resources visit the
Q: Skills for Success companion website at
www.oup.com/elt/teacher/Qskillsforsuccess

Q Teacher's Handbook gives strategic support through:

- specific teaching notes for each activity
- ideas for ensuring student participation
- multilevel strategies and expansion activities
- the answer key
- special sections on 21st Century Skills and critical thinking
- a *Testing Program CD-ROM* with a customizable test for each unit

Q Class Audio includes:

- reading texts
- *The Q Classroom*

> It's an interesting, engaging series which provides plenty of materials that are easy to use in class, as well as instructionally promising.
> *Donald Weasenforth, Collin College, Texas*

UNIT	READING	WRITING
1 **First Impressions** ❓ **How do you make a good first impression?** **READING 1:** How to Make a Strong First Impression A Magazine Article (Interpersonal Communication) **READING 2:** Job Interviews 101 A Magazine Article (Jobs and Work)	• Preview text using a variety of strategies • Read for main ideas • Read for details • Use glosses and footnotes to aid reading comprehension • Read and recognize different text types • Fill out a questionnaire to anticipate content of reading • Identify main ideas and supporting details	• Write paragraphs of different genres • Plan before writing • Revise, edit, and rewrite • Give feedback to peers and self-assess • Develop a paragraph: topic sentence, supporting sentences, concluding sentence • Make an outline • Write a "how to" paragraph
2 **Food and Taste** ❓ **What makes food taste good?** **READING 1:** Knowing Your Tastes A Magazine Article (Food) **READING 2:** Finding Balance in Food An Online Magazine Article (Nutrition)	• Preview text using a variety of strategies • Read for main ideas • Read for details • Use glosses and footnotes to aid reading comprehension • Read and recognize different text types • Take a quiz to anticipate content of reading • Analyze the structure of a text as a previewing strategy • Use prior knowledge to predict content	• Write paragraphs of different genres • Plan before writing • Revise, edit, and rewrite • Give feedback to peers and self-assess • Use descriptive adjectives • Write a descriptive paragraph
3 **Success** ❓ **What does it take to be successful?** **READING 1:** Fast Cars, Big Money A Magazine Article (Business) **READING 2:** Practice Makes ... Pain? An Online Article (Sports and Competition)	• Preview text using a variety of strategies • Read for main ideas • Read for details • Use glosses and footnotes to aid reading comprehension • Read and recognize different text types • Complete a survey to anticipate content of reading • Use an idea map to activate schema • Use headings to determine the purpose of a text • Scan to find specific information such as names, numbers, and dates • Use titles to predict content	• Write paragraphs of different genres • Plan before writing • Revise, edit, and rewrite • Give feedback to peers and self-assess • Formulate opinions, reasons, and examples • Write an opinion paragraph

VOCABULARY	GRAMMAR	CRITICAL THINKING	UNIT OUTCOME
• Match definitions • Define new terms • Learn selected vocabulary words from the Oxford 3000 and the Academic Word List • Use the dictionary to identify word forms	• Real conditionals: present and future	• Reflect on the unit • Connect ideas across texts or readings • Express ideas/reactions/opinions orally and in writing • Relate information from unit to self • Set and achieve goals • Apply unit tips and use *Q Online Practice* to become a strategic learner • Complete a T-chart to categorize information • Analyze ways to make a good first impression	• Develop a "how to" paragraph that details the steps involved in making a good impression.
• Match definitions • Define new terms • Learn selected vocabulary words from the Oxford 3000 and the Academic Word List • Use context to understand unfamiliar vocabulary	• Ordering of adjectives	• Reflect on the unit • Connect ideas across texts or readings • Express ideas/reactions/opinions orally and in writing • Relate information from unit to self • Set and achieve goals • Apply unit tips and use *Q Online Practice* to become a strategic learner • Fill in a chart to categorize information • Evaluate qualities of food	• Write a paragraph about your favorite dish using descriptive adjectives.
• Match definitions • Define new terms • Learn selected vocabulary words from the Oxford 3000 and the Academic Word List • Recognize and use adjective + preposition collocations to expand vocabulary	• Subject-verb agreement	• Reflect on the unit • Connect ideas across texts or readings • Express ideas/reactions/opinions orally and in writing • Relate information from unit to self • Set and achieve goals • Apply unit tips and use *Q Online Practice* to become a strategic learner • Fill in a chart to categorize information • Evaluate the elements of personal success	• State and support your personal perspectives in an "opinion" paragraph.

UNIT	READING	WRITING
4 **New Perspectives** **How has technology affected your life?** **READING 1: Having a Second Life** A Computer Magazine Article (Social Networking) **READING 2: Living Outside the Box** An Online Newspaper Article (Technology)	• Preview text using a variety of strategies • Read for main ideas • Read for details • Use glosses and footnotes to aid reading comprehension • Read and recognize different text types • Complete a questionnaire to anticipate content of reading • Take notes while reading to be an active reader • Use title and photos to predict content	• Write paragraphs of different genres • Plan before writing • Revise, edit, and rewrite • Give feedback to peers and self-assess • Analyze features of good/poor summaries • Write a summary • Write a personal response to the unit question
5 **Responsibility** **Why do people help each other?** **READING 1: A Question of Numbers** A News Magazine Article (Psychology) **READING 2: The Biology of Altruism** A Science Journal Article (Biology)	• Preview text using a variety of strategies • Read for main ideas • Read for details • Use glosses and footnotes to aid reading comprehension • Read and recognize different text types • Use pictures to activate schema and predict content • Make predictions about text • Use graphic organizers to review and aid comprehension	• Write paragraphs of different genres • Plan before writing • Revise, edit, and rewrite • Give feedback to peers and self-assess • State reasons and give examples to support ideas in writing • Use *because* to state reasons • Write a paragraph with reasons and examples
6 **Advertising** **Does advertising help or harm us?** **READING 1: Happiness is in the Shoes You Wear** A News Magazine Article (Advertising) **READING 2: In Defense of Advertising** An Article Based on a Canadian Radio Show (Business)	• Preview text using a variety of strategies • Read for main ideas • Read for details • Use glosses and footnotes to aid reading comprehension • Read and recognize different text types • Use photos to activate schema and anticipate content • Make predictions about text • Distinguish fact from opinion to be a critical reader • Use prior knowledge to predict content	• Write paragraphs of different genres • Plan before writing • Revise, edit, and rewrite • Give feedback to peers and self-assess • Write introduction, body, and concluding paragraphs • Write a letter to the editor based on the unit question
7 **Risk** **Why do people take risks?** **READING 1: Fear Factor: Success and Risk in Extreme Sports** An Article from *National Geographic News* (Psychology) **READING 2: The Climb of My Life** An Excerpt from a Book (Extreme Sports)	• Preview text using a variety of strategies • Read for main ideas • Read for details • Use glosses and footnotes to aid reading comprehension • Read and recognize different text types • Use photos to activate schema and anticipate content • Identify and use referents in text to understand contrast • Make predictions about text • Sequence ideas to show text structure • Use prior knowledge to predict content	• Write paragraphs of different genres • Plan before writing • Revise, edit, and rewrite • Give feedback to peers and self-assess • Write a multi-paragraph narrative essay with the focus on the introductory paragraph

VOCABULARY	GRAMMAR	CRITICAL THINKING	UNIT OUTCOME
• Match definitions • Define new terms • Learn selected vocabulary words from the Oxford 3000 and the Academic Word List • Learn and use synonyms to expand vocabulary and add variety to writing	• Parallel structure	• Reflect on the unit • Connect ideas across texts or readings • Express ideas/reactions/opinions orally and in writing • Relate information from unit to self • Set and achieve goals • Apply unit tips and use *Q Online Practice* to become a strategic learner • Compare and contrast information presented in a chart • Formulate an opinion	• Write a paragraph summarizing a reading text and an opinion paragraph in response to the text.
• Match definitions • Define new terms • Learn selected vocabulary words from the Oxford 3000 and the Academic Word List • Learn and use phrasal verbs to expand vocabulary	• Gerunds and infinitives	• Reflect on the unit • Connect ideas across texts or readings • Express ideas/reactions/opinions orally and in writing • Relate information from unit to self • Set and achieve goals • Apply unit tips and use *Q Online Practice* to become a strategic learner • Use a graphic organizer to see connections between ideas and patterns of organization • Determine what makes people help each other	• Write a paragraph about why people help others using reasons and examples.
• Match definitions • Define new terms • Learn selected vocabulary words from the Oxford 3000 and the Academic Word List • Learn and use suffixes to change word forms and expand vocabulary	• Compound sentences with *and, but, so,* and *or*	• Reflect on the unit • Connect ideas across texts or readings • Express ideas/reactions/opinions orally and in writing • Relate information from unit to self • Set and achieve goals • Apply unit tips and use *Q Online Practice* to become a strategic learner • Fill in a chart to categorize information • Formulate and justify an opinion	• Write a multiple-paragraph letter to the editor expressing your opinion about advertising.
• Match definitions • Define new terms • Learn selected vocabulary words from the Oxford 3000 and the Academic Word List • Use the dictionary to find and use the correct definition of words with multiple meanings	• Shifts between past and present in narrative writing	• Reflect on the unit • Connect ideas across texts or readings • Express ideas/reactions/opinions orally and in writing • Relate information from unit to self • Set and achieve goals • Apply unit tips and use *Q Online Practice* to become a strategic learner • Rank and justify rankings • Analyze and describe a previous personal risk	• Develop a narrative essay describing a risk you have taken.

UNIT	READING	WRITING
8 **Cities/Urban Lives** 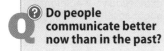 **How can we make cities better places to live?** **READING 1: New Zero-Carbon City to be Built** A News Website Article (Environmental Science) **READING 2: "Out of the Box" Ideas for Greener Cities** A News Magazine Article (City Planning)	• Preview text using a variety of strategies • Read for main ideas • Read for details • Use glosses and footnotes to aid reading comprehension • Read and recognize different text types • Take a quiz to anticipate content of reading • Make predictions about text • Make inferences to maximize comprehension	• Write paragraphs of different genres • Plan before writing • Revise, edit, and rewrite • Give feedback to peers and self-assess • Write a problem/solution essay with the focus on the thesis statement
9 **Money** **How can a small amount of money make a big difference?** **READING 1: How a Ugandan Girl Got an Education** A News Magazine Article (Charity) **READING 2: Money Makes You Happy— If You Spend It on Others** A News Website Article (Psychology)	• Preview text using a variety of strategies • Read for main ideas • Read for details • Use glosses and footnotes to aid reading comprehension • Read and recognize different text types • Use photos to activate schema and anticipate content • Use a timeline to determine the sequence of events • Make predictions about text	• Write paragraphs of different genres • Plan before writing • Revise, edit, and rewrite • Give feedback to peers and self-assess • Write a cause/effect essay with the focus on body paragraphs
10 **Communication** **Do people communicate better now than in the past?** **READING 1: 2B or not 2B?** A Newspaper Article (Communication Studies) **READING 2: Social Networking Sites: Are They Changing Human Communication?** A Magazine Article (Social Networking)	• Preview text using a variety of strategies • Read for main ideas • Read for details • Use glosses and footnotes to aid reading comprehension • Read and recognize different text types • Complete a survey to anticipate content of reading • Order details to determine sequence in text • Identify the author's purpose, audience, and tone • Use prior knowledge to predict content • Skim text for main idea	• Write paragraphs of different genres • Plan before writing • Revise, edit, and rewrite • Give feedback to peers and self-assess • Write an opinion essay with the focus on counterarguments and the concluding paragraph

VOCABULARY	GRAMMAR	CRITICAL THINKING	UNIT OUTCOME
• Match definitions • Define new terms • Learn selected vocabulary words from the Oxford 3000 and the Academic Word List • Recognize and use participial adjectives to expand vocabulary	• Passive voice	• Reflect on the unit • Connect ideas across texts or readings • Express ideas/reactions/ opinions orally and in writing • Relate information from unit to self • Set and achieve goals • Apply unit tips and use *Q Online Practice* to become a strategic learner • Categorize advantages in a chart • Identify a problem and formulate solutions	• Write a problem/solution essay describing how your city can become a better place to live.
• Match definition • Define new terms • Learn selected vocabulary words from the Oxford 3000 and the Academic Word List • Learn and use noun collocations to expand vocabulary	• Complex sentences	• Reflect on the unit • Connect ideas across texts or readings • Express ideas/reactions/opinions orally and in writing • Relate information from unit to self • Set and achieve goals • Apply unit tips and use *Q Online Practice* to become a strategic learner • Complete a graphic organizer to show cause/effect • Assess a situation and interpret cause and affect	• Write a cause/effect essay explaining how a small amount of money can make a big difference.
• Match definitions • Define new terms • Learn selected vocabulary words from the Oxford 3000 and the Academic Word List • Use prefixes to guess meaning of new vocabulary	• Sentence fragments	• Reflect on the unit • Connect ideas across texts or readings • Express ideas/reactions/opinions orally and in writing • Relate information from unit to self • Set and achieve goals • Apply unit tips and use *Q Online Practice* to become a strategic learner • Recognize arguments and counterarguments • State an opinon and justify it with reasons and examples	• Develop an essay about communication that states your personal opinion and gives a counterargument.

Unit QUESTION

How do you make a good first impression?

First Impressions

READING • identifying main ideas and supporting details
VOCABULARY • using the dictionary
WRITING • organizing and developing a paragraph
GRAMMAR • real conditionals: present and future

LEARNING OUTCOME

Develop a "how to" paragraph that details the steps involved in making a good impression.

▶ *Reading and Writing 3, pages 2–3*

Preview the Unit

Learning Outcome

1. Ask for a volunteer to read the unit skills, then the unit learning outcome.

2. Explain: *This is what you are expected to be able to do by the unit's end. The learning outcome explains how you are going to be evaluated. With this outcome in mind, you should focus on learning these skills (Reading, Vocabulary, Writing, Grammar) that will support your goal of writing a "how to" paragraph about making a good first impression. This can also help you act as mentors in the classroom to help the other students meet this outcome.*

A (15 minutes)

1. Say: *Whenever you meet someone for the first time, you want to make a good first impression.* Tell students about a time when you tried to make a good first impression. Elicit situations where people try particularly hard to make good first impressions.

2. Put students in pairs or small groups to discuss the first two questions.

3. Call on volunteers to share their ideas with the class. Ask follow-up questions: *Is it important to make a good first impression? Why or why not?*

4. Focus students' attention on the photo. Have a volunteer describe the photo to the class. Read the questions aloud and elicit answers. Ask: *Who do you think the two men are? Do you think they're both making a good impression? Why or why not?*

Activity A Answers, p. 3
Answers will vary. Possible answers:
1. honesty, kindness, intelligence, sense of humor;
2. dress nicely, smile, be polite;
3. The people are at a meeting in an office. The two men are meeting for the first time; they are going to do business together.

B (20 minutes)

1. Introduce the Unit Question, *How do you make a good first impression?* Explain to students that each unit in Q focuses on a Unit Question that they will consider throughout the unit and will address in their Unit Assignment at the end.

2. Point out that answers to this Unit Question can fall into categories: things to wear, things to say, things to do, and possibly "other."

3. Write each category at the top of one of the columns of a chart on a sheet of poster paper.

4. Give students a moment to think about their responses, and then elicit answers for the question.

5. Make notes of the answers under the correct categories. Post the chart to refer to later in the unit.

Activity B Answers, p. 3
Answers will vary. Possible answers:
Lower-level answers: wear nice clothes, smile
Mid-level answers: dress neatly, act friendly and be helpful, ask questions
Higher-level answers: show an interest in other people, be confident and relaxed

The Q Classroom (5 minutes)

CD 1, Track 2

1. Play The Q Classroom. Use the example from the audio to help students continue the conversation. Ask: *How did the students answer the question? Do you agree or disagree with their ideas? Why?*

2. Ask students to look over the chart they created for Activity B. Elicit and add to the chart any ideas from the audio that aren't already included.

▶ *Reading and Writing 3, page 4*

C (5 minutes)

Direct students to work individually to complete the questionnaire. Tell them to choose the best answer, even if it doesn't describe their situation perfectly.

D (10 minutes)

1. Have students discuss their answers with a partner.

2. Ask who thinks their partner makes a good first impression, and call on volunteers to explain why.

EXPANSION ACTIVITY: Initiating Conversation (10 minutes)

1. Part of making a good first impression is being able to talk easily with people. As a class, brainstorm questions that make good conversation starters. Write these questions on the board. Possible questions: *How do you like this weather? What do you think of this [school/class/activity]? Did you catch the news today? I like your [watch]. Can I ask where you got it? What are you planning to do this weekend? How has your week been?*

2. Conduct a mingling activity. Have the students stand and find a partner. Tell them they have 30 seconds to conduct a quick conversation with their partner using one of the questions on the board. Call time after 30 seconds and tell students to find a new partner and start a new conversation. Repeat the activity until students have spoken to four or five partners.

▶ *Reading and Writing 3, page 5*

READING

READING 1: How to Make a Strong First Impression

VOCABULARY (15 minutes)

1. Direct students to read each sentence and guess what they think the word in bold means. Then have them match the words with the definitions.

2. Put students in pairs to compare answers. Elicit the answers from volunteers.

3. Have students repeat the bold vocabulary words after you. Highlight the syllable in each word that receives primary stress.

4. Ask questions to help students connect with the vocabulary. For example: *When was the last time you talked to a **stranger**? What have you **demonstrated** to someone before?*

MULTILEVEL OPTION

Group lower-level students and assist them with the task. Provide alternate example sentences or ask questions to help them understand the words. *You have to be very good to get a job at that company—they have very high **standards**. When I **appreciate** something, I say thank you. What are some things boys do to **impress** girls? I like my weight right now—I want to **maintain** this weight.*

Have higher-level students complete the activity individually and then compare answers with a partner. Assign several words to each pair and tell them to write an additional sample sentence for each one. Have volunteers write one of their sentences on the board. Correct the sentences with the whole class, focusing on the use of the word rather than other grammatical issues.

Vocabulary Answers, p. 5
2. i; **3.** b; **4.** d; **5.** a; **6.** e;
7. g; **8.** c; **9.** j; **10.** h

 For additional practice with the vocabulary, have students visit *Q Online Practice.*

Tip for Success (3 minutes)

1. Have students read the tip aloud.

2. Explain: *Before you read, you can preview an article by reading the title, subtitle, or headings. This will give you a general idea of what the article will be about.*

3. Elicit the title and subtitles of the article. Have students share what they think the main points of the article are.

PREVIEW READING 1 (5 minutes)

1. Have students read the directions and check their predictions.

2. Tell students they should review their answers after reading.

> **Preview Reading 1 Answer, p. 6**
> (checked): show people you are interested in them

Reading 1 Background Note

Students can easily find online articles about making a good first impression. In addition to the information included in this article, many articles suggest the following: keep your body language open by not crossing your arms or legs; turn your body toward the people you are shaking hands with or talking to; stand at a comfortable distance—not too near or too far—from others; and use proper grammar and avoid slang.

Culture note: in many countries, offices have a communal coffee pot, which employees can use throughout the day. Employees are responsible for making more coffee whe they take the last cup. Not doing so is considered impolite.

READ (20 minutes)

🔊 CD 1, Track 3

1. Instruct students to read the article. Point out that they should refer to the glossed word as they read. Tell them to mark any unknown vocabulary but to continue reading. Ask them to set their pens down or look up when they've completed the article.

2. When most students have finished reading, elicit and discuss their vocabulary questions.

3. Play the audio and ask students to read along silently.

MAIN IDEAS (10 minutes)

1. Ask students to read the statements and complete the activity individually.

2. Call on volunteers for the answers.

3. Elicit corrections for false statements. Have students find the information in the reading that supports the true statements.

> **Main Idea Answers, p. 7**
> **2.** F; **3.** T; **4.** T; **5.** F

DETAILS (10 minutes)

1. Direct students to read the questions and write answers.

2. Have students compare answers with a partner.

3. Direct students to look back at the article to check their answers.

4. Go over the answers with the class.

> **Details Answers, p. 8**
> **1.** stand up straight, look other people in the eye, smile frequently;
> **2.** that meeting the person is an ordinary experience;
> **3.** People may judge your intelligence and level of cultural knowledge by how you speak. They may be bored if you speak in a monotone;
> **4.** If you look around, they'll think you don't want to talk to them;
> **5.** Try to use the name of the person you've just met;
> **6.** The other person may think you are too different.

 For additional practice with reading comprehension, have students visit *Q Online Practice*.

Critical Thinking Tip (5 minutes)

1. Have a student read the tip aloud. Explain: *We often have to explain our ideas in speaking and in writing.*

2. Ask: *In your everyday life, when do you have to explain things in detail? For example, when you call a company to make a complaint about a product, what do you have to explain? Can you think of any other examples?*

Explain Your Ideas

Point out that the *What Do You Think* activity will always ask students to write five to eight sentences in response to one question because that encourages them to explore one question in depth and explain their ideas in detail. Take the class through the process of answering the first question. Elicit and write sentences on the board, encouraging students to develop their thoughts, rather than make a list of unconnected ideas. For example: *When you meet someone for the first time, you should avoid talking about controversial topics like politics. People have different opinions about politics. If you bring up this topic right away, you might disagree with the new person.*

Q WHAT DO YOU THINK? (20 minutes)

1. Ask students to read the questions and reflect on their answers.

2. Seat students in small groups and assign roles: a group leader to make sure everyone contributes, a note-taker to record the group's ideas, a reporter to share the group's ideas with the class, and a timekeeper to watch the clock.

3. Give students five minutes to discuss the questions. Call time if conversations are winding down. Allow them an extra minute or two if necessary.

4. Call on each group's reporter to share ideas with the class.

5. Have each student choose one of the questions and write 5–8 sentences in response.

6. Call on volunteers to share their responses with the class.

MULTILEVEL OPTION

Allow lower-level students to work with partners to write three sentences in response to the question they choose.

Ask higher-level students to respond to more than one question.

What Do You Think? Answers, p. 8
Answers will vary. Possible answers:
1. religion, politics, money;
2. because people know more about themselves than about others, and people generally like to share their own experiences;

3. Yes, everyone likes people who show interest in them./No, it's more important to be an interesting person. Other ways to make a good first impression could include doing something nice for the other person or helping the other person.

Learning Outcome

Use the learning outcome to frame the purpose and relevance of Reading 1. Ask: *What did you learn from Reading 1 that will help you write a "how to" paragraph about making a good first impression?* (Students learned tips for making a good first impression that they can use in their paragraphs.)

▶ *Reading and Writing 3, page 9*

Reading Skill: Identifying main ideas and supporting details (5 minutes)

1. Ask students what a *main idea* is. Elicit the meaning of *support*, and ask students what they think *supporting details* are. Then have them read the information about main ideas and supporting details.

2. Check comprehension by asking questions: *Where can you usually find the topic sentence? What does it tell you? What do the supporting sentences contain?* Review the meanings of *skim* and *scan*. (*Skim* is reading quickly for the gist, or general idea. *Scan* is looking through the text for specific information.)

A (10 minutes)

1. Have students work individually to complete the activity.

2. Elicit the answers from volunteers.

Reading Skill A Answers, p. 9
1. a. SD; **b.** MI; **c.** SD;
2. a. SD; **b.** SD; **c.** MI;
3. a. MI; **b.** SD; **c.** SD

B (10 minutes)

1. Have students work individually to find and underline the topic sentences in paragraphs 2, 3, and 7. Then ask them to compare answers with a partner.

2. Go over the answers with the class.

For additional practice with identifying main ideas and supporting details, have students visit *Q Online Practice.*

▶ *Reading and Writing 3, page 10*

READING 2: Job Interviews 101

VOCABULARY (15 minutes)

1. Direct students to read the words and definitions in the box. Answer any questions about meaning or provide examples of the words in context.

2. Then pronounce each word and have students repeat. Highlight the syllable that receives the primary stress in each word.

3. Have students work with a partner to complete the sentences. Call on volunteers to read the completed sentences aloud. Provide feedback on pronunciation.

> **Vocabulary Answers, pp. 10–11**
> **1.** professional;   **2.** weakness;   **3.** expect;
> **4.** punctual;   **5.** responsible;   **6.** slang;
> **7.** consider;   **8.** accomplishment;
> **9.** exaggerate;   **10.** research

 For additional practice with the vocabulary, have students visit *Q Online Practice.*

▶ *Reading and Writing 3, page 11*

PREVIEW READING 2 (5 minutes)

1. Have students read the directions and check their predictions. Have them briefly discuss their answers with a partner.

2. Tell students they should review their answer after reading.

> **Preview Reading 2 Answer, p. 11**
> (checked): a

Reading 2 Background Note

Here are some additional tips to share with students about what to do during a job interview. Dressing well: If you're not sure what to wear, it's better to look too conservative than not conservative enough. Punctuality: Visit the location of your interview ahead of time so you know how long it takes to get there. Speaking: Speak in a clear, confident voice. Body language: Use a firm handshake. Asking questions: avoid questions about salary, vacations, and benefits until you've received an offer. Also, don't forget to turn off your cell phone!

READ (5 minutes)

 CD 1, Track 4

1. Instruct students to read the article. Remind them to refer to the glossed words. Tell them to mark any unknown vocabulary but to continue reading. Ask them to set their pens down or look up when they've completed the article.

2. When most students have finished reading, elicit and discuss their vocabulary questions.

3. Play the audio and ask students to read along silently.

▶ *Reading and Writing 3, page 13*

MAIN IDEAS (15 minutes)

1. Direct students to look at the T-chart. Explain what *Dos* and *Don'ts* mean. Elicit an additional example for each column.

2. Ask students to complete the activity individually.

3. Re-create the T-chart on the board and call on volunteers to help you complete it.

> **Main Ideas Answers, p. 13**
> Answers will vary. Possible answers:
>
> | Job Interview *Dos* | Job Interview *Don'ts* |
> |---|---|
> | Dress professionally. Learn about the company. Think of questions and practice. Be punctual. Make eye contact. Sit up straight. Be polite. Find shared interests. Agree with the interviewer. Talk about your accomplishments. Stay positive. Smile. Ask questions. | Don't be negative. Don't use slang or bad words. Don't interrupt. Don't exaggerate. Don't lie. Don't forget to breathe. |

DETAILS (10 minutes)

1. Direct students to read the statements and complete the activity.

2. Have students compare answers with a partner.

3. Direct the students to look back at the article to check their answers.

4. Go over the answers with the class. Elicit corrections for false statements.

Details Answers, p. 13
1. T; **2.** F; **3.** F; **4.** T; **5.** F; **6.** T; **7.** F

 For additional practice with reading comprehension, have students visit *Q Online Practice*.

▶ *Reading and Writing 3, page 14*
WHAT DO YOU THINK?

A (10 minutes)

1. Ask students to read the questions and reflect on their answers.

2. Seat students in small groups and assign roles: a group leader to make sure everyone contributes, a note-taker to record the group's ideas, a reporter to share the group's ideas with the class, and a timekeeper to watch the clock.

3. Give students five minutes to discuss the questions. Call time if conversations are winding down. Allow them an extra minute or two if necessary.

4. Call on each group's reporter to share ideas with the class.

5. Have each student choose one of the questions and write five to eight sentences in response.

6. Call on volunteers to share their responses with the class.

Activity A Answers, p. 14
Answers will vary. Possible answers:
1. I think "Dress professionally" is the most important tip because the interviewer won't even listen to what you say if you are dressed badly. If you dress neatly and professionally, it shows that you care about the impression you are making. It also shows that you will look professional if you get the job. I think talking about my accomplishments is the hardest thing to do because I always feel like I'm bragging. But I know that interviewers really want to know about my accomplishments.

2. I think the best way to make an interviewer interested in me is by giving thoughtful answers to the questions and being enthusiastic about the job. If I give thoughtful answers, it will show that I want to do my best. Employers want to hire people who are willing to work hard and do their best. If I'm enthusiastic, the interviewer will see that I really care about the job. Employers don't want to hire people who don't want to work at their companies.

B (5 minutes)

1. Tell the students that they should think about both Reading 1 and Reading 2 as they answer the questions in B.

2. Ask students to discuss their answers in their groups.

3. Call on each group to share their responses with the class.

Activity B Answers, p. 14
Answers will vary. Possible answers:
1. Dress professionally. Show interest in others by asking questions. Make eye contact.
2. Don't interrupt. Don't look around the room when someone is talking to you. Don't arrive late for appointments.
3. Yes, because it's always important to be polite and appear confident./No, because you need to be very formal at a job interview, but classmates expect you to be more informal.

Learning Outcome

Use the learning outcome to frame the purpose and relevance of Readings 1 and 2. Ask: *What did you learn from Readings 1 and 2 that prepares you to write a "how to" paragraph about making a good impression?* (Students learned tips for making a good impression generally and at job interviews. They may want to use this information in their "how to" paragraphs.)

Vocabulary Skill: Using the dictionary
(10 minutes)

1. Read the information about word families and direct students to look at the dictionary definitions.

2. Check comprehension: *Which word is a verb? noun? adjective? Are the meanings of the words similar? Are they exactly the same?*

3. Write sentences with blanks on the board and elicit the correct form of *accomplish* to complete them. *I _____ a lot last night. My friend has many _____. She is a very _____ musician.*

Skill Note

Learning word forms is a crucial step in helping students move from passive understanding of a word to using it correctly. Make a habit of pointing out the form of a new vocabulary word and teaching related forms. In many cases, different word forms have slightly different meanings, and often students don't pick up on these subtle differences just from seeing words in context.

Even higher-level students may understand the meaning of a word but be unclear on the use of different forms. Assigning additional word-form work is a great way to keep these students challenged when vocabulary exercises are easy for them.

▶ *Reading and Writing 3, page 15*

Tip for Success (2 minutes)

1. Read the Tip aloud.
2. Elicit a sentence for *tie* as a noun and as a verb. (*He wears a tie. He tied his shoelaces.*) Provide additional examples of words with the same noun and verb form: *dress, show, interest,* etc.

A (15 minutes)

1. Direct students to look at the chart and read the different forms of *accomplish*. Have them work to complete the chart, using a dictionary for help.
2. Go over the answers with the class. As you pronounce each word, highlight the syllable that receives primary stress. Point out the nouns that have a different stressed syllable from the verbs, such as *consideration* vs. *consider, demonstration* vs. *demonstrate, responsibility* vs. *responsible,* etc.

> **Activity A Answers, p. 15**
> **2.** consideration; consider;
> **3.** confident; confidently;
> **4.** demonstration; demonstrative;
> **5.** impression; impressive;
> **6.** offense; offensive;
> **7.** responsibility; responsibly;
> **8.** selection; selective; selectively

B (10 minutes)

1. Direct students to complete the sentences with the correct words from the chart. Tell them that they need to think about both the form and the meaning of the missing words to complete the sentences.
2. Call on volunteers to read the completed sentences aloud.

> **Activity B Answers, p. 15**
> **2.** consideration;   **3.** confidence;   **4.** demonstrate;
> **5.** impressive;   **6.** offend

 For additional practice with word forms, have students visit *Q Online Practice.*

C (10 minutes)

1. Model the activity with *accomplish*. Write: *My biggest accomplishment was getting my college degree. I feel good because I accomplished a lot today. You must be an accomplished musician to play in an orchestra.* Direct students to choose two of the other word families and write a sentence for each word.
2. Call on different volunteers to write a sentence on the board for each word in the chart.

> **Activity C Answers, p. 15**
> Answers will vary. Ensure that students have used word forms correctly.

▶ *Reading and Writing 3, page 16*

WRITING

Writing Skill Part 1: Organizing and developing a paragraph (20 minutes)

1. Read through the information about developing a paragraph aloud.
2. Stop after each section and check comprehension. *Should a paragraph have many ideas or should it focus on one idea? Where will you usually find the topic sentence? What is the purpose of a topic sentence? What kind of information is in the supporting sentences? What does the concluding sentence do?*

A (5 minutes)

1. Direct students to read the paragraph in the box.
2. Tell them to keep in mind the information about topic sentences, supporting sentences, and concluding sentences as they read.

B (5 minutes)

1. Direct students to circle the topic sentence of the paragraph.
2. Ask a volunteer to read the topic sentence aloud.

Activity B Answer, p. 16
(circled): When you start a job, you can leave a bad impression on your new co-workers very quickly without even realizing it.

C (5 minutes)

1. Have students look for the first supporting sentence and underline it. Elicit the sentence and discuss any confusion or differences of opinion.

2. Tell students to complete the activity individually. Ask them to compare their work with a partner.

3. Elicit any disagreements or questions from students.

Activity C Answers, p. 16
(underlined): One sure way to annoy your co-workers ... phone; Another common mistake is ... and not make another pot; Leaving your cell phone on is another way ... cause them to form a bad impression of you; (circled): Finding your dream job ... quickly and easily!

 For additional practice with organizing and developing a paragraph, have students visit *Q Online Practice*.

▶ *Reading and Writing 3, page 17*

Writing Skill Part 2: Organizing and developing a paragraph (25 minutes)

1. Read the introductory paragraph about outlines, and then ask students to read the outline.

2. Check comprehension: *What sentences should be included in an outline? Do supporting details need to be in complete sentences in the outline?*

3. Direct students to read the paragraph and work individually to complete the outline on p. 18.

4. Re-create the outline on the board and ask volunteers to complete it.

Writing Skill Part 2 Answers p. 18
Answers will vary. Possible answers:
2.A. Figure out why others are upset.
2.A.2. Did you tell a bad joke?
2.B.1. Make a plan about what to say and not to say.
2.B.2. Don't make the same mistake twice.
2.C. Be positive and interested.
2.C.2. Ask questions and pay attention.
Concluding sentence: There is no magic formula...the next time!

 For additional practice with organizing and developing a paragraph, have students visit *Q Online Practice*.

▶ *Reading and Writing 3, page 18*

Grammar: Real conditionals: present and future (10 minutes)

1. Read the information about the present real conditional. Check comprehension by providing students with *if* clauses and elicit several completions, including completions with modals. *If you arrive late to an interview, ...; If you don't look at the interviewer, ...*

2. Repeat the procedure with the future real conditional and elicit future completions for the same *if* clauses. Point out that with these "advice" sentences, either conditional is correct, but there are situations where only present or future is correct. For example, *If it rains tomorrow, I will stay home.*

3. Read the examples of conditional clauses with *when*. Elicit restatements of the previous *if* clauses with *when*. (*When you smile frequently,...*)

4. Have students look back at the examples and compare the punctuation in sentences that start with an *if* (or *when*) clause vs. the ones that end with that clause. (If the *if/when* clause follows the result clause, there is no comma.)

Skill Note

When using the future conditional, students often make the error of inserting the modal *will* in the *if* clause (*If you will arrive late...*) or of not using the present tense ending for third person verbs (*If he arrive late...*). Try some practice skeletons that require students to complete the *if* clause. (*If he/you _____, he/you won't get the job.*)

▶ *Reading and Writing 3, page 19*

A (10 minutes)

1. Ask students to read the directions and complete the activity individually.

2. Elicit the answers from volunteers.

Activity A Answers, p. 19
1. (People want to be around you) when you have good listening skills.
2. If you tell a joke (you could offend someone.)
3. When you dress appropriately, (people take you seriously.)
4. (You are more likely to make a good impression) if you are confident and prepared.
5. If you don't ask questions, (people may not think) (you're interested in what they're saying.)

B (10 minutes)

1. Ask students to read the directions and complete the activity individually.

2. Call on volunteers to read the completed sentences aloud.

> **Activity B Answers, p. 19**
> **2.** feel; **3.** will have; **4.** come; **5.** doesn't study

 For additional practice with factual conditionals, have students visit *Q Online Practice*.

▶ *Reading and Writing 3, page 20*

C (15 minutes)

1. Direct students to complete the sentences with their own ideas.

2. Ask volunteers to write their completed sentences on the board.

> **Activity C Answers, p. 20**
> Answers will vary. Possible answers:
> **1.** I will be tired;
> **2.** you might not get the job;
> **3.** he will think you don't care about him;
> **4.** you may offend someone;
> **5.** the interviewer will think you're not responsible.

MULTILEVEL OPTION

Have higher-level students write two or three additional sentences about job interviews or about making a good first impression. Tell them to use an *if* or *when* clause in each sentence.

Q Unit Assignment:
Write a "how to" paragraph

21ST CENTURY SKILLS

In any position of responsibility, whether as a manager at work, a leader of a classroom group, or a participant in a community activity, students may be called upon to give instructions to others. To do that well, they need to be able to identify steps in a process, organize them in a logical fashion, and explain them clearly. Writing a "how to" paragraph gives students valuable practice with each of those skills.

To help students make the connection between this assignment and the general value of the skill, ask them to brainstorm other situations in which they might need to explain how to do something to someone.

Unit Question (5 minutes)

Refer students back to the ideas they discussed at the beginning of the unit about making a good first impression. Tell them they can use the ideas from their chart to help them write their Unit Assignment paragraph. Cue students if necessary by asking specific questions about the content of the unit: *What should you do to make a good impression? How should you speak? What should you wear? How can you make a good impression at a job interview? At a new job? In a new class?*

Learning Outcome

1. Tie the Unit Assignment to the unit learning outcome. Say: *The outcome for this unit is to write a "how to" paragraph. This Unit Assignment is going to let you show your skill in planning and organizing a paragraph and using the present and future conditional.*

2. Explain that you are going to use a rubric similar to their Self-Assessment checklist on page 22 to grade their Unit Assignment. You can also share a copy of the Unit Assignment Rubric (on p. 12 of this *Teacher's Handbook*) with the students.

Plan and Write

Brainstorm

A (15 minutes)

1. Ask students to read the possible topics in the chart. Point out that they can choose their own topic, but it shouldn't be "an interviewer."

2. Direct students to complete the T-chart with ideas they might use in their paragraphs. Monitor and provide feedback as students work.

▶ *Reading and Writing 3, page 21*

Plan

B (15 minutes)

1. Review the functions of a topic sentence, supporting sentences, and a concluding sentence. Refer students to the outlines on pages 17 and 18.

2. Have students work individually to complete their outlines. Monitor and provide feedback.

▶ *Reading and Writing 3, page 22*

Write

C (15 minutes)

1. Direct students to look at the Self-Assessment checklist on p. 22. Go over each item with the class. Remind students that you will be using a similar rubric to evaluate their writing.

2. Ask students to work individually to write their paragraphs.

Alternative Unit Assignments

Assign or have students choose one of these assignments to do instead of, or in addition to, the Unit Assignment.

1. Write a paragraph about a time someone made a very good first impression or a very bad first impression on you. Make some suggestions for the future based on what you learned from this experience.

2. Brainstorm with a partner what a person should do to make a good first impression on a customer, patient, or student. Write a list of tips.

 For an additional Unit Assignment, have students visit *Q Online Practice*.

Revise and Edit

Peer Review

A (15 minutes)

1. Pair students and direct them to read each other's work.

2. Ask students to answer the questions and discuss them.

3. Give students suggestions for how to give helpful feedback: *I like your ideas about what to say. Do you think you could add an example about body language?*

Rewrite

B (10 minutes)

Students should review their partners' answers from Activity A and rewrite their paragraphs if necessary.

Edit

C (10 minutes)

1. Direct students to read and complete the Self-Assessment checklist. They should be prepared to hand in their work or discuss it in class.

2. Ask for a show of hands for how many students gave all or mostly *yes* answers.

3. Use the Unit Assignment Rubric on p. 12 in this *Teacher's Handbook* to score each student's assignment.

4. Alternatively, divide the class into large groups and have students read their paragraphs to their group. Pass out copies of the Unit Assignment Rubric and have students grade each other.

▶ *Reading and Writing 3, page 23*

Track Your Success (5 minutes)

1. Have students circle the words they have learned in this unit. Suggest that students go back through the unit to review any words they have forgotten.

2. Have students check the skills they have mastered. If students need more practice to feel confident about their proficiency in a skill, point out the page numbers and encourage them to review.

3. Read the Learning Outcome aloud. Ask students if they feel that they have met the outcome.

Unit Assignment Rubric

Student name: _____

Date: _____

Unit Assignment: *Write a "how to" paragraph about how to make a good first impression.*

20 points = Paragraph element was completely successful (at least 90% of the time).
15 points = Paragraph element was mostly successful (at least 70% of the time).
10 points = Paragraph element was partially successful (at least 50% of the time).
 0 points = Paragraph element was not successful.

"How to" Paragraph	20 points	15 points	10 points	0 points
Student used correct spelling and punctuation.				
Student used correct word forms.				
Paragraph includes vocabulary from the unit.				
Paragraph clearly explains how to make a good first impression.				
Student included conditionals and used them correctly.				

Total points: _____

Comments:

Unit QUESTION
What makes food taste good?

Food and Taste

READING • previewing a text
VOCABULARY • use of context to understand words
WRITING • using descriptive adjectives
GRAMMAR • use and placement of adjectives

LEARNING OUTCOME

Write a paragraph about your favorite dish using descriptive adjectives.

▶ *Reading and Writing 3, pages 24–25*
Preview the Unit

Learning Outcome

1. Ask for a volunteer to read the unit skills, then the unit learning outcome.

2. Explain: *This is what you are expected to be able to do by the unit's end. The learning outcome explains how you are going to be evaluated. With this outcome in mind, you should focus on learning these skills (Reading, Vocabulary, Writing, Grammar) that will support your goal of writing a descriptive paragraph about your favorite dish. This can also help you act as mentors in the classroom to help the other students meet this outcome.*

A (15 minutes)

1. Ask students what they have eaten so far today and whether they enjoyed it a lot, a little, or not at all.

2. Put students in pairs or small groups to discuss the first two questions.

3. Call on volunteers to share their ideas with the class. Ask follow-up questions: *What's your favorite food that you eat every day? What's your favorite food to eat on a special occasion? Do you like the same foods your family and friends do, or do you like some unusual things? Do you prefer salty, sweet, spicy, or sour foods?*

4. Focus students' attention on the photo. Have a volunteer describe the photo to the class. Read the question aloud and elicit responses. Ask: *Is there anything in the photo you've never tasted? Is there anything you really like or don't like? Do you use these foods in cooking? How?*

Activity A Answers, p. 25
Answers will vary. Possible answers:
1. rice, soup, sandwiches, beans, etc.;
2. tamales, bulgolgi, cake, etc.;
3. Yes, I think presentation affects how food tastes. I think that if food looks delicious, you expect it to taste delicious, so it does./No, I don't think presentation is important. I think food served on a paper plate tastes the same as food served on fancy china.

B (20 minutes)

1. Read the Unit Question aloud. Tell the students, *Let's start off our discussion by listing our ideas about what makes food taste good.*

2. Seat students in small groups and direct them to title a piece of paper: *What makes food taste good?* Have them pass around the paper as quickly as they can, with each group member adding one idea to the list. Tell them they have two minutes to make the lists and write as many ideas as possible.

3. Call time and ask a reporter from each group to read the list aloud.

4. Use items from the lists as a springboard for discussion. For example, *Many groups wrote something about fresh ingredients on their list. Why are fresh ingredients so important?*

Activity B Answers, p. 25
Answers will vary. Possible answers:
Lower-level answers: sugar, salt, spices
Mid-level answers: homemade, fresh ingredients
Higher-level answers: nicely arranged (presented), pleasant memories

The Q Classroom (5 minutes)

🔊 CD 1, Track 5

1. Play The Q Classroom. Use the example from the audio to help students continue the conversation. Ask: *How did the students answer the question? Do you agree or disagree with their ideas? Why?*

2. Ask students to look over the lists they created for Activity B. Elicit and add to the lists any ideas from the audio that aren't already included.

▶ *Reading and Writing 3, page 26*

C (5 minutes)

1. Go over any essential vocabulary in the quiz, such as *snack, appetizer,* and *dessert.* Direct students to work individually to complete the quiz.

D (10 minutes)

1. Direct students to discuss their answers with a partner.

2. Call on volunteers to explain how their answers were different from their partners' answers.

EXPANSION ACTIVITY: Continue the Quiz (20 minutes)

1. Have students continue working with their partners from Activity D. Tell the partners to come up with three additional questions for the food quiz. (For example: *What kind of ____ do you prefer?* + three answer choices.) Monitor and provide feedback while partners are working.

2. Direct partners to ask their new questions of at least three classmates.

3. Have partners report to the class what they learned about their classmates.

▶ *Reading and Writing 3, page 27*

READING

READING 1:
Knowing Your Tastes

VOCABULARY (15 minutes)

1. Direct students to read the words and definitions in the box. Answer any questions about meaning or provide examples of the words in context. Pronounce each word and have students repeat. Highlight the syllable in each word that receives the primary stress.

2. Have students work individually to complete the sentences. Have students compare answers with a partner. Call on volunteers to read the completed sentences aloud.

3. Have the pairs read the sentences together.

MULTILEVEL OPTION

Group lower-level students and assist them with the task. Provide alternate example sentences or questions to help them understand the words. *A **balanced** meal includes different kinds of foods. Jin always comes to class; it is very **likely** that he will come tomorrow. This class **is made up of** students from many countries. If you don't study, you're **at risk** of failing your test.*

Have higher-level students complete the activity individually and then compare answers with a partner. Assign two or three words to each pair and ask them to write original sentences with the words. Have volunteers put one of their sentences on the board.

Vocabulary Answers, p. 27
1. recognize; **2.** is made up of; **3.** system;
4. likely; **5.** typically; **6.** sensitive;
7. balanced; **8.** at risk; **9.** identify

🌐 For additional practice with the vocabulary, have students visit *Q Online Practice.*

▶ *Reading and Writing 3, page 28*

PREVIEW READING 1 (5 minutes)

1. Read the directions. Ask students to describe the photos and read the subheadings aloud. Elicit what they know about the topic.

2. Write some of their ideas on the board for review after reading.

Preview Reading 1 Answer, p. 28
Answers will vary. Students may or may not know that there are different kinds of tasters, such as supertasters and nontasters.

Reading 1 Background Note

The phenomenon of taste sensitivity was discovered in the 1930s, when researchers found that people had different reactions to the chemical PTC (phenylthiocarbamide). Some people found the chemical to be horribly bitter, and others couldn't taste it at all. The term "supertaster" was coined in

1991 by Linda Bartoshuk. She noticed that people with extreme taste sensitivity had a large number of taste receptor cells (or taste buds).

READ (20 minutes)

 CD 1, Track 6

1. Instruct students to read the article. Remind them to refer to the glossed words. Tell them to mark any unknown vocabulary but to continue reading. Ask them to set their pens down or look up when they've completed the article.

2. When most students have finished reading, elicit and discuss their vocabulary questions.

3. Play the audio and ask students to read along silently.

▶ *Reading and Writing 3, page 29*

MAIN IDEAS (5 minutes)

1. Ask students to read and complete the activity individually. Have students mark the information in the text that helped them answer each question.

2. Call on volunteers for the answers.

> **Main Ideas Answers, pp. 29–30**
> **1.** b; **2.** a; **3.** b; **4.** a

▶ *Reading and Writing 3, page 30*

DETAILS (10 minutes)

1. Direct students to read the questions and write answers.

2. Have students compare answers with a partner.

3. Direct the students to look back at the article to check their answers.

4. Go over the answers with the class.

> **Details Answers, p. 30**
> **1.** sweet, sour, bitter, salty;
> **2.** 5,000 (or half the number that medium tasters have);
> **3.** a woman from Korea;
> **4.** bitter, fatty, sweet, spicy;
> **5.** Because their tastes may cause them to make unhealthy choices. Supertasters might avoid healthy vegetables. Nontasters might eat too much fat.

 For additional practice with reading comprehension, have students visit *Q Online Practice*.

▶ *Reading and Writing 3, page 31*

Q WHAT DO YOU THINK? (20 minutes)

1. Ask students to read the questions and reflect on their answers.

2. Seat students in small groups and assign roles: a group leader to make sure everyone contributes, a note-taker to record the group's ideas, a reporter to share the group's ideas with the class, and a timekeeper to watch the clock.

3. Give students five minutes to discuss the questions. Call time if conversations are winding down. Allow them an extra minute or two if necessary.

4. Call on each group's reporter to share ideas with the class.

5. Have each student choose one of the questions and write five to eight sentences in response.

6. Call on volunteers to share their responses with the class.

> **MULTILEVEL OPTION**
>
> Seat students in mixed-ability groups so that lower-level students can benefit from listening to higher-level students.
>
> Allow lower-level students to write three sentences in response to the question they choose.
>
> Ask higher-level students to respond to more than one question.

What Do You Think? Answers, p. 31
Answers will vary. Possible answers:
1. I think I'm a nontaster because I eat everything. I like very spicy food. I also like very sweet and fatty foods. My favorite foods are desserts and fried foods. I also like strong coffee.
2. I really like strawberries because they are sweet. They taste good fresh, and they're also good in pie or jam. When they are ripe, they taste like candy. I also like them because I know they are good for me. They are full of vitamin C.
3. People like foods they grew up eating or foods that remind them of happy times. Sometimes it's hard to like food that's different from the food you grew up eating. If a food looks strange or unusual, people might not like it. People often dislike foods that have made them sick. They might also dislike foods that they had to eat a lot when they were young. For example, when I was young, my mother made me eat broccoli all the time. Now I don't like it.

Learning Outcome

Use the learning outcome to frame the purpose and relevance of Reading 1. Ask: *What did you learn from Reading 1 that will help you write a descriptive paragraph about food?* (Students learned about different kinds of tasters. They may use this information when they write about their own taste preferences.)

READING 2: Finding Balance in Food

VOCABULARY (15 minutes)

1. Direct students to read the sentences and cross out the answer choice that is different from the bold word.

2. Put students in pairs to compare answers. Elicit the answers from volunteers. Have students repeat the bold vocabulary words. Highlight the syllable that receives the primary stress in each word.

3. Ask questions to help students connect with the vocabulary: *What foods do you think we consume the most in this country? Who or what has influenced your food choices? Name a region of the United States/of your native country.*

> **Vocabulary Answers, pp. 31–32**
> Crossed out:
> **2.** a;   **3.** b;   **4.** c;   **5.** a;   **6.** b;
> **7.** b;   **8.** c;   **9.** b;   **10.** a

 For additional practice with the vocabulary, have students visit *Q Online Practice*.

▶ *Reading and Writing 3, page 32*
Reading Skill: Previewing a text (5 minutes)

1. Elicit the meaning of *preview* and ask students what they think it means to preview a text. Then direct them to read the information in the box.

2. Check comprehension by asking questions: *Why is it a good idea to preview a text before you read it? What should you read to preview a text? What information should you learn from previewing?* Point out that this skill is particularly useful when having to read long or difficult texts, such as textbook chapters or documents written with specialized vocabulary.

A (15 minutes)

1. Have students work individually to follow Steps 1, 2, and 3 and answer the questions.

2. Ask students to compare their responses with a partner.

> **Reading Skill A Answers, pp. 32–33**
> **Step 1:** 1. Finding Balance in Food; 2. Food, Balance, and Culture; France: Balancing Geography and Portions; China: Balancing Yin and Yang; Different Cultures, Shared Desire;
> **Step 2:** food regions of France; yin-yang symbol;
> **Step 3:** (underlined): 1st paragraph– Nutritionists around the world...a balanced diet.; Last paragraph– France and China have very different cultures, and people in each culture have their own ideas of what constitutes a balanced meal...benefits.

▶ *Reading and Writing 3, page 33*
B (10 minutes)

1. Ask students to write in their own words what they think the topic of the reading is.

2. Elicit ideas from a couple of volunteers to demonstrate that different wording of the same idea is fine.

> **Reading Skill B Answer, p. 33**
> Answers will vary. Possible answers:
> how different cultures define a balanced diet; how France and China have different definitions of a balanced diet

C (10 minutes)

Tell students to answer the question using the information they gained by previewing the reading.

> **Reading Skill C Answer, p. 33**
> food and culture; different definitions of a balanced diet

 For additional practice with previewing a text, have students visit *Q Online Practice*.

PREVIEW READING 2 (5 minutes)

1. Have students read the directions. Elicit what they already know about the topic.

2. Tell students they should review their ideas after reading.

> **Preview Reading 2 Answer, p. 33**
> Answers will vary. Students may know, from their own experience or from previewing the text, that different cultures have different ideas about a balanced diet; they may have ideas about how a balanced diet is defined in their own culture.

Reading 2 Background Note

Although different cultures have different ideas of a balanced diet, nutritionists have found commonalities among cultures considered to have healthy diets (including French and Chinese cuisine). These commonalities are: 1. Eat a lot of produce and whole grains; 2. Eat slowly; 3. Control portions; 4. Eat unprocessed, fresh food; 5. Use herbs and spices.

READ (20 minutes)

 CD 1, Track 7

1. Instruct students to read the article. Remind students to refer to the glossed words. Tell them to mark any unknown vocabulary but to continue reading. Ask them to set their pens down or look up when they've completed the article.

2. When most students have finished reading, elicit and discuss their vocabulary questions.

3. Play the audio and ask students to read along silently.

▶ *Reading and Writing 3, page 35*
MAIN IDEAS (10 minutes)

1. Ask students to read and complete the activity individually.

2. Elicit the answers from the class. Have students point out the information in the text that helped them answer each question.

> **Main Ideas Answers, p. 35**
> **1.** a; **2.** b; **3.** b; **4.** a; **5.** c

▶ *Reading and Writing 3, page 36*
DETAILS (10 minutes)

1. Direct students to read the statements and complete the activity individually.

2. Go over the answers with the class. Elicit corrections for the false sentences.

> **Details Answers, p. 36**
> **1.** T; **2.** F; **3.** F; **4.** T; **5.** F; **6.** T

 For additional practice with reading comprehension, have students visit *Q Online Practice*.

Q WHAT DO YOU THINK?

A (10 minutes)

1. Ask students to read the questions and reflect on their answers.

2. Seat students in small groups and assign roles: a group leader to make sure everyone contributes, a note-taker to record the group's ideas, a reporter to share the group's ideas with the class, and a timekeeper to watch the clock.

3. Give students five minutes to discuss the questions. Call time if conversations are winding down. Allow them an extra minute or two if necessary.

4. Call on each group's reporter to share ideas with the class.

5. Have each student choose one of the questions and write five to eight sentences in response.

6. Call on volunteers to share their responses with the class.

> **Activity A Answers, p. 36**
> Answers will vary. Possible answers:
> **1.** I prefer to eat more variety because it keeps my diet interesting. Different kinds of foods have different nutrients. I eat small portions because I need to limit the number of calories I eat. I also like to enjoy many different flavors in one meal. I usually eat more than three times a day, but I only eat a little at each meal.
> **2.** I like the Chinese food called chow mein. It has a lot of noodles and vegetables and sometimes meat or chicken. Chinese dishes never have cheese or bread. In my country, we eat a lot of beans, cheese, meat, and bread. I like our food the best, but I think Chinese food is healthier.

B (15 minutes)

1. Tell the students that they should think about Reading 1 and Reading 2 as they answer the questions in Activity B.

2. Ask students to discuss their answers in their groups.

3. Call on each group to share their responses with the class.

> **Activity B Answers, p. 36**
> Answers will vary. Possible answers:
> **1.** I like food that is homemade with fresh ingredients. I also like salty food.
> **2.** I didn't like fish when I was a child, but now I love it. I liked hot dogs when I was young, but now I think they're disgusting. I think food preferences change as you get older because you learn more about food.

Learning Outcome

Use the learning outcome to frame the purpose and relevance of Readings 1 and 2. Ask: *What did you learn from Readings 1 and 2 that will help you write a descriptive paragraph about food?* (Students learned about different kinds of tasters and different definitions of a balanced diet. They may want to use this information when they write their descriptive paragraphs.)

21ST CENTURY SKILLS

The ability to solve problems is an essential skill that employers want their employees to have, and it's also an important skill to use throughout school and life. Figuring out the meaning of words from context is a problem-solving skill because it requires students to think carefully about what they are reading and draw conclusions. Point out to students that making the effort to use context clues to understand unknown words will help them deal with different texts they may encounter on the job or at school.

▶ *Reading and Writing 3, page 37*

Vocabulary Skill: Use of context to understand words (5 minutes)

1. Direct students to read the first paragraph about context. Write the example sentence on the board. Help students identify the context, or words around the bold word, that help define *consuming*. Then read through the rest of the information together.

2. Check comprehension by asking questions: *What is context? How can you tell that* consuming *means "eating" in this sentence? What can you do if you read a word in a text that you don't know?*

Skill Note

Some students are anxious about encountering words they don't understand and feel that it's necessary to look up every word in the dictionary. Point out that there are two very important skills to work on: reading and vocabulary building. If students stop to look up each word they don't know, they train themselves to become slow word-by-word readers, which is bad for their reading comprehension.

Tell students to make a habit of marking words that they want to look up as they read. Explain that they should avoid looking words up while reading unless not knowing the word makes it hard to understand the passage. Sometimes the context will make the meaning of the word clear, and when it doesn't, they can look the words up later, at which time their focus can be on learning vocabulary rather than on understanding a text.

A (15 minutes)

1. Direct students to read the sentences and attempt to answer the questions without using a dictionary for help.

2. Go over the answers with the class.

> **Activity A Answers, pp. 37–38**
> **2.** beef with broccoli and sweet and sour chicken;
> **3.** They can be soft or hard.
> **4.** They like sugary foods.
> **5.** according to the way a dish tastes or how a meal is prepared and served;
> **6.** yin and yang foods

▶ *Reading and Writing 3, page 38*

B (10 minutes)

1. Direct students to complete the activity individually.

2. Call on volunteers for the answers. Elicit the context clues that helped them understand the underlined words.

> **Activity B Answers, p. 38**
> **1.** b; **2.** a; **3.** a; **4.** b; **5.** a; **6.** b

C (10 minutes)

1. Direct students to write four sentences with different words from Activities A and B.

2. Have students write one or two sentences on the board for each word. Help students with any errors in word use.

> **Activity C Answers, p. 38**
> Answers will vary. Possible answers:
> My family cooks many dishes for Chinese New Year. I have a taste for sweet foods, so I love chocolate. Fried octopus has a chewy texture.

 For additional practice with use of context to understand words, have students visit *Q Online Practice*.

WRITING

Writing Skill: Using descriptive adjectives (20 minutes)

1. Read aloud the information about using adjectives in writing. Discuss the meanings of *delicious, savory,* and *cozy.*

2. Check comprehension. Ask: *Why do writers use adjectives? What do* delicious *and* savory *describe in this sentence? What does* cozy *describe?*

A (5 minutes)

1. Ask students if they know what a Yorkshire pudding is. Show them a picture of one from the Internet. Direct students to read the paragraph in the box. Then have partners work together to complete the activity.

2. Elicit the answers from the class.

> **Activity A Answers, p. 39**
> **1.** (underlined): <u>Whenever I think of my mother's cooking, I always remember her delicious Yorkshire puddings.</u>
> **2.** (underlined): <u>Yorkshire pudding is such a simple and common English food, but it will always be special to me because of my mother.</u>
> **3.** (circled) My mother's Yorkshire puddings taste so good because they are light, crisp, and slightly sweet.

B (10 minutes)

1. Have students continue working with their partners from Activity A. Tell them to look through the paragraph to find the adjectives.

2. Elicit the adjectives from volunteers. Discuss their meanings.

> **Activity B Answers, p. 40**
> delicious, traditional, simple, light, crisp, sweet, special, homemade, common, English

 For additional practice with using descriptive adjectives in writing, have students visit *Q Online Practice.*

Grammar: Use and placement of adjectives (10 minutes)

1. Read the information about the use and placement of adjectives and ask students to look at the chart. Elicit the types of the adjectives in the example sentences (e.g., *big* = size; *old* = age).

2. Check comprehension by asking: *How many adjectives should you use before a noun (at most)? If you want to add a fourth adjective, what should you do?*

Skill Note

The adjective-order chart can be a useful way of recording new vocabulary. Have students copy the chart into their notebooks, and direct them to write any new adjectives they learn in the chart. If they can't find a place for a new word in the chart, it can be a springboard for discussion of the correct use and placement of the new word. If you have space in the classroom, you may want to make a large classroom version of the chart to post on a bulletin board for recording new adjectives and referencing adjective order throughout the semester.

A (10 minutes)

1. Ask students to work with a partner to write the adjectives in the chart. Students may want to copy the chart into their notebooks rather than writing in the book.

2. Elicit the answers from volunteers.

> **Activity A Answers, pp. 40–41**
> Opinion/Quality: pretty, funny, lovely, tasty, interesting, common, friendly, ugly, cheap, fashionable, uncomfortable, unusual, traditional, wonderful, nice, elegant
> Size: little, huge
> Age: modern, antique, teenage, elderly, ancient
> Shape: oval, rectangular, triangular
> Color: orange
> Origin: Korean, Brazilian, Omani, American
> Material: glass, wool, cotton, plastic, metal, silk, ceramic
> Kind/Purpose: wedding, dancing, hiking, medical, writing, racing

Critical Thinking Tip (5 minutes)

1. Have a student read the tip aloud. Explain: *We often classify things in our lives to help us organize things and information.*

2. Ask: When do you have to classify things in your everyday life? For example, think about how you organize your clothing. Do you put certain types of clothing together? Can you think of other things you classify?

Critical Q: Expansion Activity

Classify Foods

Point out that the reason for classifying adjectives is to know what they describe about an object and the order to use them in. To encourage students to think more about classification and to build vocabulary for the Unit Assignment paragraph about food, ask them to talk with a partner for two minutes about how they classify the food in their kitchen cabinets. Ask: *Which foods do you store near each other? Why? What do you store on the lower shelves? What do you store on the higher shelves?* Ask partners if they had different ways of classifying their food.

▶ *Reading and Writing 3, page 41*

B (10 minutes)

1. Ask students to work individually to write the sentences. Monitor and provide feedback.

2. Have volunteers write one of their sentences on the board.

Activity B Answers, p. 41
Answers will vary. Possible sentences:
1. I like the delicious, traditional, Italian dessert called tiramisu.
2. I have a funny, friendly, little brother named Carlos.
3. I'm wearing a comfortable, large, cotton t-shirt.
4. I ate a cheap, delicious Mexican meal at Rosie's Café.
5. I watched a sad, old, American movie last night.
6. Domenico's is an elegant, expensive, Italian restaurant.

MULTILEVEL OPTION

Allow lower-level students to write just the adjectives + noun phrase (e.g., *cheap, delicious, Mexican meal*) or to include only two adjectives (e.g., *old American movie*). Have volunteers write one of their ideas on the board. Discuss with the class how to integrate the phrase into a sentence.

 For additional practice with use and placement of adjectives, have students visit *Q Online Practice*.

▶ *Reading and Writing 3, page 42*

Unit Assignment:
Write a descriptive paragraph

Unit Question (5 minutes)

Refer students back to the ideas they discussed at the beginning of the unit about what makes food taste good. Tell them they can use the ideas to help them write their Unit Assignment paragraph. Cue students if necessary by asking specific questions about the content of the unit: *What makes food taste delicious? What would you consider a balanced meal? What adjectives can you use to describe food?*

Learning Outcome

1. Tie the Unit Assignment to the unit learning outcome. Say: *The outcome for this unit is to write a descriptive paragraph. This Unit Assignment is going to let you show your skill in using descriptive adjectives to write about your favorite dish.*

2. Explain that you are going to use a rubric similar to their Self-Assessment checklist on page 44 to grade their Unit Assignment. You can also share a copy of the Unit Assignment Rubric (on p. 22 of this *Teacher's Handbook*) with the students.

Plan and Write

Brainstorm

A (15 minutes)

Ask students to read the questions and write answers in their notebooks. Remind them that at this point they are just trying to get ideas—they can answer the questions in note form and shouldn't worry about writing perfect sentences.

▶ *Reading and Writing 3, page 43*

Plan

B (15 minutes)

1. Review the functions of a topic sentence, supporting sentences, and a concluding sentence.

2. Have students work individually to complete their outlines. Monitor and provide feedback.

Write

C (15 minutes)

1. Read the writing directions aloud. Remind students that you are going to use a rubric similar to their Self-Assessment checklist on p. 44 to grade their Unit Assignment. Go over the checklist with the class.

2. Ask students to work individually to write their paragraphs.

Alternative Unit Assignments

Assign or have students choose one of these assignments to do instead of, or in addition to, the Unit Assignment.

1. Imagine your perfect restaurant. Make a list of food items that you would include on the menu. Write a short description of each item.

2. In your culture, what special food do you eat on certain holidays or at celebrations? Write a descriptive paragraph about it.

 For an additional Unit Assignment, have students visit *Q Online Practice*.

▶ *Reading and Writing 3, page 44*

Revise and Edit

Peer Review

A (15 minutes)

1. Pair students and direct them to read each other's work.

2. Ask students to answer the questions and discuss them.

3. Give students suggestions for how to give helpful feedback: *This sounds delicious. Maybe you can say whether it is sweet, salty, or spicy.*

Rewrite

B (10 minutes)

Students should review their partners' answers from A and rewrite their paragraphs if necessary.

Edit

C (10 minutes)

1. Direct students to read and complete the Self-Assessment checklist. They should be prepared to hand in their work or discuss it in class.

2. Ask for a show of hands for how many students gave all or mostly *yes* answers.

3. Use the Unit Assignment Rubric on p. 22 in this *Teacher's Handbook* to score each student's assignment.

4. Alternatively, divide the class into large groups and have students read their paragraphs to their group. Pass out copies of the Unit Assignment Rubric and have students grade each other.

▶ *Reading and Writing 3, page 45*

Track Your Success (5 minutes)

1. Have students circle the words they have learned in this unit. Suggest that students go back through the unit to review any words they have forgotten.

2. Have students check the skills they have mastered. If students need more practice to feel confident about their proficiency in a skill, point out the page numbers and encourage them to review.

3. Read the Learning Outcome aloud. Ask students if they feel that they have met the outcome.

Unit 2   Food and Taste

Unit Assignment Rubric

Student name: _____

Date: _____

Unit Assignment: *Write a descriptive paragraph about your favorite dish.*

20 points = Paragraph element was completely successful (at least 90% of the time).
15 points = Paragraph element was mostly successful (at least 70% of the time).
10 points = Paragraph element was partially successful (at least 50% of the time).
 0 points = Paragraph element was not successful.

Descriptive Paragraph	20 points	15 points	10 points	0 points
The paragraph is well organized.				
Student used correct spelling.				
Paragraph includes vocabulary from the unit.				
Student used descriptive adjectives to describe a favorite dish.				
Adjectives are in the correct order.				

Total points: _____

Comments:

Unit QUESTION
What does it take to be successful?

Success

READING • scanning a text
VOCABULARY • collocations
WRITING • organizing an opinion paragraph
GRAMMAR • subject-verb agreement

LEARNING OUTCOME

State and support your personal perspectives in an "opinion" paragraph.

▶ *Reading and Writing 3, pages 46–47*
Preview the Unit

Learning Outcome

1. Ask for a volunteer to read the unit skills, then the unit learning outcome.

2. Explain: *This is what you are expected to be able to do by the unit's end. The learning outcome explains how you are going to be evaluated. With this outcome in mind, you should focus on learning these skills (Reading, Vocabulary, Writing, Grammar) that will support your goal of writing an opinion paragraph about what it takes to be successful. This can also help you act as mentors in the classroom to help the other students meet this outcome.*

A (15 minutes)

1. Ask students whom they would describe as successful and why they think that person is successful.

2. Put students in pairs or small groups to discuss the first two questions.

3. Call on volunteers to share their ideas with the class. Ask follow-up questions: *Is the success worth the sacrifice? Do you know anyone who sacrificed a lot in order to be successful?*

4. Focus students' attention on the photo. Have a volunteer describe the photo to the class. Read the question aloud. Ask: *How does she feel? Why?* Ask if any of the students like to watch speed skating.

Activity A Answers, p. 47
Answers will vary. Possible answers:
1. by working hard and practicing; by having talent, a good coach, or opportunities;
2. time with family and friends, other interests, free time;
3. She's lying on the ice. She probably just lost a race.

B (20 minutes)

1. Introduce the Unit Question: *What does it take to be successful?* Ask related information questions or questions about personal experience to help students prepare for answering the more abstract unit question.

2. Put students in small groups and give each group a piece of poster paper and a marker.

3. Read the Unit Question aloud. Give students a minute to silently consider their answers to the question.

4. Tell students to pass the paper and the marker around the group. Direct each group member to write a different answer to the question. Encourage them to help one another.

5. Ask each group to choose a reporter to read the answers to the class. Discuss similarities and differences among each group's answers. If answers from different groups are similar, make a group list that incorporates all of the answers. Post the list to refer to later in the unit.

Activity B Answers, p. 47
Answers will vary. Possible answers:
Lower-level: hard work, practice, talent, sacrifice
Mid-level: ambition, the ability to focus on what you want, being willing to sacrifice
Higher-level: (Students may be able to support their answers with an anecdote about a successful person they know.) You have to work hard to be successful. My uncle has a very successful company, but he spent many years working night and day to build it.

The Q Classroom (5 minutes)
🔊 CD 1, Track 8

1. Play The Q Classroom. Use the example from the audio to help students continue the conversation. Ask: *How did the students answer the question? Do you agree or disagree with their ideas? Why?*

2. Ask students to look over the answers they wrote for Activity B. Elicit and add any ideas from the audio that aren't already included.

▶ *Reading and Writing 3, page 48*

C (5 minutes)

1. Have students read the directions and look at the chart. Ask them to work individually to check the column that reflects their opinion about each statement.

2. Direct students to discuss their answers with a partner. Then call on volunteers to share their ideas with the class. Elicit reasons for their opinions.

EXPANSION ACTIVITY: Talk about Sports (10 minutes)

To get students ready for writing about their favorite sport in Activity D, have them discuss the following questions in small groups:

What sport do you think is the most dangerous?

What sport do you think is the most expensive?

What sport do you think is the most difficult?

What's your favorite sport to watch? To play?

How often do you watch or play it?

What Olympic sports do you like to watch on TV?

What sport do you hate to watch on TV?

Critical Thinking Tip (2 minutes)

1. Have a student read the tip aloud. Explain: *There are several different kinds of diagrams we can use to organize our ideas.*

2. Ask: *What kind of diagram is in Activity D? Does it help you compare two things? What does it help you do?*

D (10 minutes)

1. Have students look at the idea map. Model filling out the idea map on the board. Elicit a favorite sport from a volunteer and examples of financial costs, physical costs, and emotional costs for that sport. Explain that *costs* has a similar meaning to *sacrifices*.

2. Ask students to work individually to complete their maps and then to discuss their ideas with a partner.

MULTILEVEL OPTION

Group lower-level students and elicit their favorite sports. Have them work together to brainstorm financial, physical, and emotional costs for each sport. Ask questions to help students think about the costs, such as *Does the sport cost a lot of money? Can you get hurt? Do you have to spend time away from your family or friends?*

Activity D Answers, p. 48
Answers will vary. Possible answers:
My Favorite Sport: gymnastics
Financial Costs: training fees, travelling to competitions, special clothing
Physical Costs: injuries, long hours of training, straining the body
Emotional Costs: can't spend time with friends and family, sometimes have to move away from family for training, difficult when you lose a competition

▶ *Reading and Writing 3, page 49*

READING

READING 1: Fast Cars, Big Money

VOCABULARY (15 minutes)

1. Work through the first item together. Read the sentence, replacing *logo* with each of the choices to show students which answer makes sense. Students may do the same for the remaining items.

2. Direct students to read the sentences and circle the word with the same meaning as the bold word.

3. Put students in pairs to compare answers. Elicit the answers from volunteers. Have students repeat the vocabulary words. Highlight the syllable in each bold word that receives primary stress.

4. Ask questions to help students connect with the vocabulary: *Do you have any **logos** on your clothes or on items you are carrying? Think about a sport you watch—where do you see the **sponsors'** names?*

Vocabulary Answers, p. 49
2. support;
3. sure;
4. income;
5. spend;
6. number of customers;
7. strength;
8. reliable;
9. growth;
10. appearance

 For additional practice with the vocabulary, have students visit *Q Online Practice*.

PREVIEW READING 1 (5 minutes)

1. Have students read the directions and headings in the article. Then have them choose their prediction.

2. Tell them they should review their answer after reading.

> **Preview Reading Answer, p. 50**
> Checked: to encourage businesses to invest in car racing

▶ *Reading and Writing 3, page 50*

Reading 1 Background Note

Formula 1 car racing began in Europe, but it has spread throughout the world and is watched on TV by millions of people. The Formula 1 season consists of a series of races, called Grand Prix, that are held in different countries. The winners of the Grand Prix compete in two World Championships, one for the drivers and one for the constructors (teams that build the car chassis). Have students look at photos that accompany the article. Ask if they are familiar with or if they follow Formula 1.

READ (20 minutes)

 CD 1, Track 9

1. Instruct students to read the article. Remind them to reference the glossed words. Tell them to mark any unknown vocabulary but to continue reading. Ask them to set their pens down or look up when they've completed the article.

2. When most students have finished reading, elicit and discuss their vocabulary questions.

3. Play the audio and ask students to read along silently.

▶ *Reading and Writing 3, page 51*

MAIN IDEAS (10 minutes)

1. Ask students to read each paragraph and think about the main idea. Then have them choose the sentence that best reflects the main idea.

2. Call on volunteers for the answers.

> **Main Ideas Answers, p. 51**
> **b.** 3; **c.** 2; **d.** 4; **e.** 5

DETAILS (10 minutes)

1. Direct students to read each question and cross out the incorrect answer. Emphasize that three of the answers are correct.

2. Go over the answers with the class. Point out the information in the text that helps you know why each answer is incorrect.

> **Details Answers, pp. 51–52**
> Crossed out: **1.** b; **2.** a; **3.** d

 For additional practice with reading comprehension, have students visit *Q Online Practice*.

▶ *Reading and Writing 3, page 52*

WHAT DO YOU THINK? (20 minutes)

1. Ask students to read the questions and reflect on their answers.

2. Seat students in small groups and assign roles: a group leader to make sure everyone contributes, a note-taker to record the group's ideas, a reporter to share the group's ideas with the class, and a timekeeper to watch the clock.

3. Give students five minutes to discuss the questions. Call time if conversations are winding down. Allow them an extra minute or two if necessary.

4. Call on each group's reporter to share ideas with the class.

5. Have each student choose one of the questions and write five to eight sentences in response.

6. Call on volunteers to share their responses with the class.

What Do You Think? Answers, p. 52

Answers will vary. Possible answers:

1. I think it's a good investment. So many people see the ads. People all over the world watch the races. A company that sponsors Formula 1 racing would become known around the world. That would help improve their profits.

2. I think they would find other ways to advertise. Sponsoring sports isn't the only way to reach a global market. Companies can also advertise on television and in magazines. Another thing they can do is give away samples of their products so people can try them out. If people try out a product and like it, they will buy it.

Learning Outcome

Use the learning outcome to frame the purpose and relevance of Reading 1. Ask: *What did you learn from Reading 1 that will help you write an opinion paragraph about what it takes to be successful?* (Students learned about how companies achieve success through sponsorship of a sport. They may want to keep this information in mind when they write their paragraphs.)

Reading Skill: Scanning a text (5 minutes)

1. Direct students to read the information about scanning.

2. Check comprehension by asking questions: *What is scanning? What kind of information do you scan for? What kinds of materials do we scan? How would you scan for dates?*

A (10 minutes)

1. Direct students to read number 1. Ask what kinds of words they will be looking for when they scan for the missing information (names of businesses). Tell them to keep that idea in their minds as they scan for the missing information.

2. Ask students to hold up their hand when they've found the answers. When most students have their hands up, elicit the answers and ask students to write them in the blanks.

3. Repeat the procedure with each sentence, encouraging students to identify key words and visualize what they are looking for before they scan.

Reading Skill A Answers, pp. 52–53

1. banks, hotels, telecommunications companies;
2. doors, hood, trunk;
3. the Middle East, Asia;
4. Bahrain, Abu Dhabi, Singapore

▶ *Reading and Writing 3, page 53*

B (10 minutes)

1. Tell students to scan the reading again, this time looking for numbers to complete the sentences.

2. Elicit the answers from volunteers.

Reading Skill B Answers, p. 53

1. 350;   **2.** tens, millions;   **3.** $5 million; $30 milion;
4. $300 million

 For additional practice with scanning a text, have students visit *Q Online Practice.*

READING 2: Practice Makes ... Pain?

VOCABULARY (15 minutes)

1. Direct students to read the sentences and look at the words in bold. Have students circle the word that best matches the bold word.

2. Call on volunteers to read the completed sentences aloud.

3. Ask questions to check comprehension of the words: *What are some other **demanding** activities? What's a popular **trend** today? Finish this sentence: [famous person's] success is **due to** ____.*

Vocabulary Answers, pp. 53–54
1. a; **2.** b; **3.** a; **4.** b; **5.** a;
6. b; **7.** c; **8.** a; **9.** b

For additional practice with the vocabulary, have students visit *Q Online Practice.*

▶ *Reading and Writing 3, page 54*

PREVIEW READING 2 (5 minutes)

1. Discuss the title of the article. Ask if students know the original expression, *Practice makes perfect.*

2. Have students read the directions and check their predictions.

3. Tell students they should review their answer after reading.

> **Preview Reading 2 Answer, p. 54**
> (checked): The sacrifices children make for success in sports are sometimes too great.

Reading 2 Background Note

Many experts believe that organized sports help keep children in good physical shape as well as develop their social skills, self-discipline, and maturity. So it's not surprising that twenty million children each year register for competitive sports.

However, 70% of the kids who sign up for a sport quit playing it by the time they are 13. Experts suggest that part of the reason for this is that sports are no longer fun for children because there is so much emphasis on winning and excellence over simple enjoyment.* While the majority of kids drop out of sports, among the ones who remain there are growing numbers of sports-related injuries. Over 3.5 million children are treated for sports-related injuries each year, a large number of these "overuse" injuries resulting from kids pushing themselves (or being pushed) too hard.

-from "Why Most Kids Quit Sports": Carleton Kendrick Ed.M., LCSW; Family Education: http://life.familyeducation.com/sports/behavior/29512.html

READ (5 minutes)

 CD 1, Track 10

1. Instruct students to read the article. Remind them to refer to the glossed words. Tell them to mark any unknown vocabulary but to continue reading. Ask them to set their pens down or look up when they've completed the article.

2. When most students have finished reading, elicit and discuss their vocabulary questions.

3. Play the audio and ask students to read along silently.

▶ *Reading and Writing 3, page 56*

MAIN IDEAS (15 minutes)

1. Direct students to read each statement and try to finish it. Then have them find the information in the text that helps them complete each statement.

2. Ask students to compare answers with a partner.

> **Main Ideas Answers, p. 56**
> Answers will vary. Possible answers:
> **1.** more and more children are participating in organized team competitions;
> **2.** overuse;
> **3.** they require hours of practice and game time;
> **4.** paying attention to their bodies

DETAILS (10 minutes)

1. Direct students to read the chart and think about what information they are scanning for (sport, person's name, etc.).

2. Have students work individually to scan the article and complete the chart.

3. Go over the answers with the class.

> **Details Answers, p. 56**
> **1.** Sport: gymnastics; Injury: separated cartilage in elbow;
> **2.** Name: Danny Clark; Home: Altamonte Springs, Florida; Injury: torn rotator cuff;
> **3.** Name: Kevin Butcher; Home: Fort Collins, Colorado; Sport: soccer

 For additional practice with reading comprehension, have students visit *Q Online Practice.*

Q WHAT DO YOU THINK?

A (15 minutes)

1. Ask students to read the questions and reflect on their answers.

2. Seat students in small groups and assign roles: a group leader to make sure everyone contributes, a note-taker to record the group's ideas, a reporter to share the group's ideas with the class, and a timekeeper to watch the clock.

3. Give students five minutes to discuss the questions. Call time if conversations are winding down. Allow them an extra minute or two if necessary.

4. Call on each group's reporter to share ideas with the class.

5. Have each student choose one of the questions and write five to eight sentences in response.

6. Call on volunteers to share their responses with the class.

> **Activity A Answers, p. 57**
> Answers will vary. Possible answers:
> **1.** I think sports are good for children because children get exercise and learn social skills. Playing sports can build confidence and teach teamwork. Sports can also help children stay healthy. When I was young, I was on a soccer team. Playing soccer is one of my happiest childhood memories.
> **2.** Parents and coaches have a responsibility to protect children. Children can suffer long-term injuries from sports. Children may not be mature enough to know when they should stop. They may not realize that they are overdoing it. Parents and coaches should pay attention to make sure they are not practicing too hard or too long.

B (5 minutes)

1. Have students continue working with their group from Activity A. Tell the students that they should think about both Reading 1 and Reading 2 as they answer the questions.

2. Ask students to read their sentences with a partner.

3. Call on each pair to share one of their responses with the class.

> **Activity B Answers, p. 57**
> Answers will vary. Possible answers:
> **1.** Athletes pay for success by damaging their bodies. Many athletes suffer when they are older from injuries they got when they played sports.

2. Parents of child athletes spend a lot of money on their children. They also spend a lot of time taking their children to practices and games. It can be stressful for parents to watch their children work so hard and lose their competitions.

Learning Outcome

Use the learning outcome to frame the purpose and relevance of Readings 1 and 2. Ask: *What did you learn from Readings 1 and 2 that prepares you to write an opinion paragraph about what it takes to be successful?* (Students learned about the advantages of companies being involved in sports [investing in Formula 1 racing]. However, they also learned about the disadvantages of being involved in sports at an early age and the injuries that children acquire. They may want to use this information when they write their opinion paragraphs.)

Vocabulary Skill: Collocations (15 minutes)

1. Have students read the adjective + preposition combinations.

2. Check comprehension by eliciting sample sentences with the collocations. For example, *I'm interested in science.*

Skill Note

There are dozens of adjective + preposition combinations in English. Tell students that when they are learning a new adjective, they should make a note of any preposition it's commonly used with.

Also point out that in most cases, prepositions are followed by nouns, which means they'll need to use gerunds, not verbs. Put examples on the board: *interested in politics, interested in learning; famous for his movies, famous for winning an award.*

Tip for Success (2 minutes)

1. Read the tip aloud.

2. Show students an entry from a collocations dictionary, such as *the Oxford Collocations Dictionary for Students of English,* if you have one available.

3. Explain that a collocations dictionary can help them see which words are commonly used together (not just adjectives and prepositions). For example, with the word *success*, they will find the adjectives *considerable, enormous, limited,* etc. and the verbs *achieve, enjoy, lead to,* etc.

A (15 minutes)

1. Direct students to read the adjective + preposition collocations in the box and work individually to complete the sentences.

2. Call on volunteers to read the completed sentences aloud.

   Activity A Answers, pp. 57–58
   2. due to;   **3.** sure about;   **4.** upset about;
   5. famous for;   **6.** involved in;   **7.** interested in;
   8. nervous about

▶ *Reading and Writing 3, page 58*

B (10 minutes)

1. Direct students to work individually to write sentences with the adjective + preposition collocations.

2. Call on volunteers to write their completed sentences on the board.

   Activity B Answers, p. 58
   Answers will vary. Possible answers:
   I'm very involved in my schoolwork. Gandhi was famous for his peaceful protests. She was upset about failing her test.

 For additional practice with collocations, have students visit *Q Online Practice*.

▶ *Reading and Writing 3, page 59*

WRITING

21ST CENTURY SKILLS

Employers value employees with the communication skills and critical thinking skills to organize an argument. An employee can have excellent reasons and examples to support an opinion, but if he or she can't put them in a logical order, the argument will lack coherence. Point out to students that the simple outline on p. 60 (opinion statement + reason + example to support reason) could come in handy whether they are trying to persuade their manager to rearrange the products in the store, discuss with their boss the issue of a raise, or convince the city council to put in a new stoplight.

Writing Skill: Organizing an opinion paragraph (20 minutes)

1. Direct students to read the information about writing an opinion paragraph.

2. Check comprehension: *How should you begin your opinion paragraph? What should your reasons and examples do? How should your paragraph end?*

A (5 minutes)

1. Direct students to read the paragraph in the box.

2. Tell them to underline the topic sentence and check the supporting reasons and examples.

   Activity A Answers, p. 59
   (underlined): <u>Kung fu is the perfect sport for young children.</u> (checked): Reason: it does not cost much to participate; Examples: uniform is less than fifty dollars, weekly lessons are not expensive; Reason: children learn the benefits of discipline and setting goals; Examples: colored belts keep kids motivated, child is able to succeed at his or her own pace; Reason: Kung fu teaches children how to protect themselves in the real world; Example: children… acquire important moves and motions they can use to defend themselves.

▶ *Reading and Writing 3, page 60*

B (5 minutes)

1. Direct students to complete the outline using information from the paragraph.

2. Ask students to compare their answers with a partner.

3. Elicit the answers from volunteers or re-create the outline on the board.

   Activity B Answers, p. 60
   1. Topic Sentence: Kung fu is the perfect sport for young children.
   2. Example: a typical uniform is less than fifty dollars. Reason 2: Children learn the benefits of discipline and setting goals. Example: The colored belts for completing a level keep kids motivated. Reason 3: It teaches children how to protect themselves in the real world. Example: Children acquire important moves and motions they can use to defend themselves.
   3. Concluding sentence: For these reasons, parents should consider Kung fu as a sport for their children.

 For additional practice with organizing an opinion paragraph, have students visit *Q Online Practice*.

Critical Q: Expansion Activity

Provide Valid Reasons

Make sure students see that supporting their opinions with reasons is a critical thinking skill, not just a writing skill. Write several statements on the board that students are likely to have strong opinions about, for example: *Twenty one should be the legal driving age; High school students should wear uniforms to school; Governments should provide free university education; In English class, it's more important to study grammar than conversation.*

Have students briefly discuss the statements with a partner and come up with at least two reasons for or against each one. Elicit their opinions and reasons and write them on the board. Discuss which reasons are the most compelling and which don't work. Students may come up with reasons that are not very strong, such as simple contradictions (*Grammar is not important.*) or restatements of the opinion (*Everyone needs to study grammar.*). Or they may suggest reasons that are too vague (*Twenty one is too old*).

Grammar: Subject-verb agreement

(10 minutes)

1. Read the information about subject-verb agreement with singular subjects. Elicit additional simple present statements from students.

2. Repeat the procedure with plural subjects and with the verb *be.*

3. Elicit any other collective nouns the students know. Possibilities include: *class, family, audience, society.*

Skill Note

Subject-verb agreement for students at this level tends to be a proofreading issue. Train students to check for subject-verb agreement by putting their pen (or cursor) on each verb and checking for its subject. They will often be able to catch their own mistakes if they take a systematic approach to looking for them.

▶ *Reading and Writing 3, page 61*

A (10 minutes)

1. Ask students to read the paragraph.

2. As they find errors in subject-verb agreement, have students identify what the subject is and what the verb is. Then have them correct the mistakes.

3. Elicit the corrections from volunteers.

Activity A Answers, p. 61
days are; dancers need; dancer who does; ice dancing costs; This makes; Ice dancing is; dancers do; dancers get; sacrifices are

Tip for Success (2 minutes)

1. Read the tip aloud.

2. After students have made the corrections to the paragraph in Activity A, go through it again and elicit the correct pronoun replacement for the subject in each mistake. For example, instead of *dancers needs—they need.*

▶ *Reading and Writing 3, page 62*

B (10 minutes)

1. Ask students to read the directions and complete the activity individually. Then have them compare their answers with a partner.

2. Call on volunteers to read the completed sentences aloud. Help students identify whether each subject is singular or plural. Remind students to pronounce the third-person *s.*

Activity B Answers, p. 62
2. has;
3. is;
4. need;
5. make;
6. are;
7. costs;
8. practices

 For additional practice with subject-verb agreement, have students visit *Q Online Practice.*

Q Unit Assignment:
Write an opinion paragraph

Unit Question (5 minutes)

Refer students back to the ideas they wrote down at the beginning of the unit about what it takes to be successful. Tell them they can use the ideas to help them write their Unit Assignment paragraph. Cue students if necessary by asking specific questions about the content of the unit: *What kinds of success did the Formula 1 article talk about? What were the costs of success discussed in the article about children and sports?*

Read the possible topics and elicit possible supporting arguments and examples for each one.

Learning Outcome

1. Tie the Unit Assignment to the unit learning outcome. Say: *The outcome for this unit is to write an opinion paragraph. This Unit Assignment is going to let you show your skill in organizing an opinion paragraph using correct adjective + preposition collocations and correct subject-verb agreement.*

2. Explain that you are going to use a rubric similar to their Self-Assessment checklist on p. 64 to grade their Unit Assignment. You can also share a copy of the Unit Assignment Rubric (on p. 33 of this *Teacher's Handbook*) with the students.

▶ *Reading and Writing 3, page 63*

Plan and Write

Brainstorm

A (10 minutes)

1. Ask students to work individually to write their opinion about one of the topics and brainstorm any related ideas.

2. Emphasize that at this stage they should write down every idea that comes to them.

Plan

B (15 minutes)

1. Direct students to look through the ideas they brainstormed in Activity A and circle any that support the opinion they expressed.

2. Have students work individually to complete the outline. Monitor and provide feedback.

▶ *Reading and Writing 3, page 64*

Write

C (15 minutes)

1. Direct students to look at the Self-Assessment checklist on p. 64. Remind them that you will be using a similar rubric to evaluate their writing.

2. Ask students to work individually to write their paragraphs.

Alternative Unit Assignments

Assign or have students choose one of these assignments to do instead of, or in addition to, the Unit Assignment.

1. Do you think individual or group sports help children succeed in life? Write a paragraph that supports your opinion with reasons and examples.

2. Write a paragraph about a sport or activity you did as a child. Do you think doing this sport or activity had more positive or negative effects on your life?

 For an additional Unit Assignment, have students visit *Q Online Practice*.

Revise and Edit

Peer Review

A (15 minutes)

1. Pair students and direct them to read each other's work.

2. Ask students to answer the questions and discuss them.

3. Give students suggestions for how to give helpful feedback: *This is a good reason, but I think you need an example to support it.*

Rewrite

B (10 minutes)

Students should review their partners' answers from A and rewrite their paragraphs accordingly.

Edit

C (10 minutes)

1. Direct students to read and complete the Self-Assessment checklist. They should be prepared to hand in their work or discuss it in class.

2. Ask for a show of hands for how many students gave all or mostly *yes* answers.

3. Use the Unit Assignment Rubric on p. 33 in this *Teacher's Handbook* to score each student's assignment.

4. Alternatively, divide the class into large groups and have students read their paragraphs to their group. Pass out copies of the Unit Assignment Rubric and have students grade each other.

▶ *Reading and Writing 3, page 65*

Track Your Success (5 minutes)

1. Have students circle the words they have learned in this unit. Suggest that students go back through the unit to review any words they have forgotten.

2. Have students check the skills they have mastered. If students need more practice to feel confident about their proficiency in a skill, point out the page numbers and encourage them to review.

3. Read the Learning Outcome aloud. Ask students if they feel that they have met the outcome.

Unit Assignment Rubric

Student name: _____

Date: _____

Unit Assignment: *Write an opinion paragraph about what it takes to be successful.*

20 points = Paragraph element was completely successful (at least 90% of the time).
15 points = Paragraph element was mostly successful (at least 70% of the time).
10 points = Paragraph element was partially successful (at least 50% of the time).
　0 points = Paragraph element was not successful.

Opinion Paragraph	20 points	15 points	10 points	0 points
Student used correct punctuation and spelling.				
Paragraph includes vocabulary from the unit.				
Student clearly expressed an opinion about success and provided reasons and examples to support it.				
Adjective + preposition collocations are used correctly.				
Subject-verb agreement is used correctly.				

Total points: _____

Comments:

Unit QUESTION
How has technology affected your life?

New Perspectives

READING • taking notes
VOCABULARY • synonyms
WRITING • writing a summary
GRAMMAR • parallel structure

LEARNING OUTCOME

Write a paragraph summarizing a reading text and an opinion paragraph in response to the text.

▶ *Reading and Writing 3, pages 66–67*
Preview the Unit

Learning Outcome

1. Ask for a volunteer to read the unit skills, then the unit learning outcome.

2. Explain: *This is what you are expected to be able to do by the unit's end. The learning outcome explains how you are going to be evaluated. With this outcome in mind, you should focus on learning these skills (Reading, Vocabulary, Writing, Grammar) that will support your goal of writing a summary and an opinion paragraph about how technology has affected your life. This can also help you act as mentors in the classroom to help the other students meet this outcome.*

A (15 minutes)

1. Elicit examples of technology to get students thinking about the topic. List the examples on the board.

2. Put students in pairs or small groups to discuss the first two questions.

3. Call on volunteers to share their ideas with the class. Ask follow-up questions: *Do you feel like you need your phone? Your computer? How important to you are they?*

4. Focus students' attention on the photo. Have a volunteer describe the photo to the class. Read the question aloud.

Activity A Answers, p. 67
Answers will vary. Possible answers:
1. watch TV, play a sport, talk to friends, go to movies, shop;
2. to make phone calls, take pictures/video, listen to music, watch TV/movies, write emails and texts;
3. a digital camera and a laptop; he may be uploading photos and listening to music, or he may be watching a video from his camera on his computer

B (20 minutes)

1. Introduce the Unit Question, *How has technology affected your life?* Say, *Let's consider the positive and negative effects of technology on our lives. What are some advantages of technology? What are some disadvantages?* Give students a moment to think about their answers.

2. Write *Advantages* and *Disadvantages* at the top of two sheets of poster paper.

3. Elicit students' ideas and write them in the correct categories. Post the lists to refer to later in the unit.

Activity B Answers, p. 67
Answers will vary. Possible answers:
Lower-level: good communication; fast travel; too much time at the computer
Mid-level: easier to stay in touch with people; instant access to information and entertainment; less time out with friends
Higher-level: (Students may be able to compare the use of technology today with the past.) People used to pay a lot of money to talk to friends and family who lived far away, but now they can communicate online for almost nothing. When children spend too much time at the computer, they don't get enough exercise.

The Q Classroom (5 minutes)
CD 1, Track 11

1. Play The Q Classroom. Use the example from the audio to help students continue the conversation. Ask: *How did the students answer the question? Do you agree or disagree with their ideas? Why?*

2. Ask students to look over the lists of advantages and disadvantages from Activity B. Elicit and add any ideas from the audio that aren't already included.

▶ Reading and Writing 3, page 68

C (5 minutes)

1. Have students read the directions and look at the questionnaire.

2. Ask them to work individually to check their answers. Then have them discuss their answers with a partner.

EXPANSION ACTIVITY:
Electronic Entertainment (5 minutes)

Conduct a class discussion to go into more depth about how students spend their time online and/or what they watch on TV. Find out what services they use for communication (phone or Internet), what websites they like to visit, and/or what TV shows they like to watch. Discuss the exposure to English they get from the various activities: Are they reading/ listening to native-speaker English, conversational English, formal English, etc.? Suggest ways they can increase the variety of English they're exposed to (for example, by reading news online as well as chatting, or by watching TV dramas/comedies as well as nature shows.)

D (10 minutes)

1. Have students read the chart and the questions and then discuss their answers with a partner.

2. Elicit answers to the questions from volunteers.

> **Activity D Answers, p. 68**
> Answers will vary. Possible answers:
> **1.** I spend the same amount of time watching TV. I spend much more time listening to the radio.
> **2.** I'm surprised that peple in Thailand spend so much time watching TV.

▶ Reading and Writing 3, page 69

READING

READING 1: Having a Second Life

VOCABULARY (15 minutes)

1. Direct students to read the words and definitions in the box. Answer questions about meaning or provide examples of the words in context. Then ask students to complete the sentences with the words from the box.

2. Put students in pairs to compare answers. Elicit the answers from volunteers. Have students repeat the vocabulary words. Highlight the syllable in each word that receives primary stress.

3. Ask questions to help students connect with the vocabulary: *What **benefits** do you get from studying English? Who do you **interact** with during the day? When you were young, did your parents put **limitations** on your phone use?*

MULTILEVEL OPTION

Group lower-level students and assist them with the task. Provide alternate example sentences or questions to help them understand the words. *In dry places, there is a **limitation** on how much water you can use during summer. A wedding is a **social** event. Some credit cards charge a **transaction** fee every time you use them outside the country.*

Have higher-level students complete the activity individually and then compare answers with a partner. Tell the pairs to write an additional sample sentence for each word. Have volunteers write one of their sentences on the board. Correct the sentences with the whole class, focusing on the use of the word rather than other grammatical issues.

Vocabulary Answers, p. 69
1. realistic;   **2.** explore;   **3.** virtual;
4. transaction;   **5.** interact;   **6.** social;
7. fantasy;   **8.** benefit;   **9.** limitation

 For additional practice with the vocabulary, have students visit *Q Online Practice*.

▶ Reading and Writing 3, page 70

PREVIEW READING 1 (5 minutes)

1. Have students read the first sentence of each paragraph and write their answer to the question.

2. Tell them they should review their answer after reading.

> **Preview Reading 1 Answer, p. 70**
> Answers will vary. Possible answers: to escape the stress of daily life; to live out fantasies; to interact with others

Reading 1 Background Note

Second Life was launched in 2003 and by January of 2010, had millions of accounts registered. Many different languages are supported on Second Life, and in some locations, machine translators allow residents who speak different languages to communicate with each other.

Although much media attention has been given to universities offering classes in Second Life, it is difficult to ascertain just how many universities offer classes on the site. Many universities own land in Second Life but do not offer classes there, and some Second Life universities do not have real-life counterparts.

▶ *Reading and Writing 3, page 71*

READ (20 minutes)

)) CD 1, Track 12

1. Instruct students to read the article. Remind students to refer to the glossed words. Tell them to mark any unknown vocabulary they encounter but to continue reading. Ask them to set their pens down or look up when they've completed the article.

2. When most students have finished reading, elicit and discuss their vocabulary questions.

3. Play the audio and ask students to read along silently.

▶ *Reading and Writing 3, page 72*

MAIN IDEAS (10 minutes)

1. Ask students to read the sentences. Students should refer back to paragraphs 2–6 in the article to find the main idea of each one. Then have them number the main ideas in the order that they appear in the article.

2. Go over the answers with the class.

> **Main Ideas Answers, p. 72**
> **a.** 3; **b.** 5; **c.** 1; **d.** 4; **e.** 2

DETAILS (10 minutes)

1. Direct students to work individually to read the questions and write answers. Have them look for details in each paragraph to answer the questions.

2. Have students discuss their answers with a partner. Then go over the answers with the class.

> **Details Answers, p. 72**
> **1.** by renting or selling land that they own;
> **2.** shopping malls, clubs, stores, concerts, games, conferences, art shows;
> **3.** visit an island, go skiing, fly to another planet
> **4.** There are embassies, business meetings, and college classes.
> **5.** Students can visit the campus and take classes.

 For additional practice with reading comprehension, have students visit *Q Online Practice.*

▶ *Reading and Writing 3, page 73*

WHAT DO YOU THINK? (20 minutes)

1. Ask students to read the questions and reflect on their answers.

2. Seat students in small groups and assign roles: a group leader to make sure everyone contributes, a note-taker to record the group's ideas, a reporter to share the group's ideas with the class, and a timekeeper to watch the clock.

3. Give students five minutes to discuss the questions. Call time if conversations are winding down. Allow them an extra minute or two if necessary.

4. Call on each group's reporter to share ideas with the class.

5. Have each student choose one of the questions and write five to eight sentences in response.

6. Call on volunteers to share their responses with the class.

> **MULTILEVEL OPTION**
>
> Seat students in mixed-ability groups so that lower-level students can benefit from listening to higher-level students.
>
> Allow lower-level students to write three sentences in response to the question they choose.
>
> Ask higher-level students to respond to more than one question.

What Do You Think? Answers, p. 73
Answers will vary. Possible answers:
1. One positive effect is it allows people to communicate over long distances. It provides entertainment and relaxation and it includes learning opportunities. It provides realistic online classes and business meetings. One negative effect is it may encourage people to not interact in real life. It's a world controlled by a company—not governed democratically. People may be misled by avatars that are nothing like their real-world counterparts.

2. No, I think joining is a waste of time. People should spend more time with their real friends and family rather than socializing with avatars online. Many people don't spend enough time with their families. Something like Second Life can make them spend even less time with real people. Also, I don't think it's right to spend real money on fake things, like virtual real estate.

Learning Outcome

Use the learning outcome to frame the purpose and relevance of Reading 1. Ask: *What did you learn from Reading 1 that will help you write a summary and response about the effects of technology?* (Students learned about some advantages of joining the website Second Life. They may want to include some of this information in their summary and opinion paragraph.)

Reading Skill: Taking notes (5 minutes)

1. Ask students if they usually take notes while they read. Discuss how taking notes can help them better understand a text. Direct students to read the information about taking notes.

2. Check comprehension by asking questions: *Why should you take notes? What should you underline or highlight? What types of words should you focus on? How can you remember the main idea of a paragraph?*

A (10 minutes)

1. Direct students to read the paragraph and look at the student's notes. Ask them to work individually to answer the questions.

2. Call on volunteers for the answers. Discuss their ideas.

> **Reading Skill A Answers, pp. 73–74**
> **1.** topics, main ideas, details, nouns, adjectives;
> **2.** They are background information or very specific details;
> **3.** the main idea;
> **4.** Main idea: Today's online environments have become more complex and realistic. It's stated in the topic sentence and supported by the details about Second Life.

 Reading and Writing 3, page 74

B (10 minutes)

1. Tell students to read the article again, underlining important ideas and taking notes in the margins. Ask them to compare their notes and underlining with a partner.

2. Discuss any differences the partners came up with in their comparisons.

> **Reading Skill B Answers, p. 74**
> Answers will vary. Ensure that students have underlined important ideas and have summarized main ideas in the margins.

 For additional practice with taking notes, have students visit *Q Online Practice.*

READING 2: Living Outside the Box

VOCABULARY (15 minutes)

1. Direct students to read the words and definitions in the box. Answer questions about meaning or provide examples of the words in context. Pronounce and have students repeat the words. Highlight the syllable in each word that receives primary stress.

2. Have students work with a partner to complete the sentences. Call on volunteers to read the completed sentences aloud. Provide feedback on pronunciation.

3. Ask questions to help students connect with the vocabulary: *What is something you couldn't **survive** without? What are special **occasions** in your family or country? How does someone feel when they **regret** something?*

> **Vocabulary Answers, p. 75**
> **1.** confession;
> **2.** discover;
> **3.** survive;
> **4.** occasion;
> **5.** rare;
> **6.** experiment;
> **7.** Eventually;
> **8.** regret;
> **9.** lifestyle

For additional practice with the vocabulary, have students visit *Q Online Practice.*

▶ *Reading and Writing 3, page 75*

PREVIEW READING 2 (5 minutes)

1. Discuss the title of the article and the idiom *Thinking outside the box* (thinking in new and different ways). The title is also a play on the word *box*, which is sometimes used to refer to TV.

2. Have students read the title and look at the photographs and then check their prediction.

3. Tell students they should review their prediction after reading.

> **Preview Reading 2 Answer, p. 75**
> (checked): positive

Reading 2 Background Note

People in the United States watch about 19 hours of television a week, and the viewing habits of many other countries are not that far behind. There have been numerous studies about the effects of television viewing, many of which have shown a link between heavy television viewing and poor health and diseases such as Type II diabetes. Other studies have linked television violence to violent behavior in children. Although many TV-watching studies focus on children, one study found that older adults watch more TV than younger people and enjoy it less.

-from "Older Folks Watch More TV, Get Less Out of It," Jenifer Goodwin; *Health Day*, 7/1/2010

(http://www.businessweek.com/lifestyle/content/healthday/640678.html)

▶ *Reading and Writing 3, page 76*

READ (5 minutes)

 CD 1, Track 13

1. Instruct students to read the article. Remind them to refer to the glossed words. Tell them to mark any unknown vocabulary but to continue reading. Ask them to set their pens down or look up when they've completed the article.

2. When most students have finished reading, elicit and discuss their vocabulary questions.

3. Play the audio and ask students to read along silently.

▶ *Reading and Writing 3, page 77*

MAIN IDEAS (15 minutes)

1. Ask students to read the sentences. Then have them go back to the article and find these main ideas. Students should number the main ideas in the order that they appear in the reading.

2. Go over the answers with the class.

> **Main Ideas Answers, p. 77**
> **a.** 3; **b.** 1; **c.** 4; **d.** 2

▶ *Reading and Writing 3, page 78*

DETAILS (10 minutes)

1. Direct students to read the statements and mark them *T* or *F*.

2. Call on volunteers for the answers. Elicit corrections for the false sentences.

> **Details Answers, p. 78**
> **2.** F ~~family~~ friends;
> **3.** T;
> **4.** T;
> **5.** F ~~every few months~~ almost every week;
> **6.** F ~~She is sure~~ She is *not* sure

 For additional practice with reading comprehension, have students visit *Q Online Practice*.

WHAT DO YOU THINK?

A (15 minutes)

1. Ask students to read the questions and reflect on their answers.

2. Seat students in small groups and assign roles: a group leader to make sure everyone contributes, a note-taker to record the group's ideas, a reporter to share the group's ideas with the class, and a timekeeper to watch the clock.

3. Give students five minutes to discuss the questions. Call time if conversations are winding down. Allow them an extra minute or two if necessary.

> **Activity A Answers, p. 78**
> Answers will vary. Possible answers:
> **1.** Yes, because I'd like to have time for other activities./ No, because I don't watch much TV anyway (or because I enjoy TV).
> **2.** I could not live without my computer because I use it for everything. I couldn't give up my cell phone because that's how I stay in touch with my friends and family.

B (5 minutes)

1. Tell the students that they should think about both Reading 1 and Reading 2 as they discuss the questions in Activity B. Students will choose one of the questions and write five to eight sentences in response.

2. Ask students to read their sentences with a partner.

3. Call on each pair to share their responses with the class.

> **Activity B Answers, p. 78**
> Answers will vary. Possible answers:
> **1.** Technology can help people do their work more easily and quickly. It can also help people communicate. You can be connected with friends around the world in a few seconds. But technology can take people away from interacting with others in the real world. Sometimes people spend more time online than they do talking with friends and family.
> **2.** Visiting friends is more enjoyable than online chatting because you can see their faces. People express a lot with their faces and their bodies, which you can't see online. Also, you can have different experiences when you actually see your friends. For example, you can go to concerts or for walks in the park. Or you can go on trips together and see new places. When you chat online, you're just sitting in front of your computer, and that's not very exciting.

Learning Outcome

Use the learning outcome to frame the purpose and relevance of Readings 1 and 2. Ask: *What did you learn from Readings 1 and 2 that prepares you to write a summary and response about the effects of technology?* (In the two readings, students learned about some positive effects of using technology frequently as well as some advantages of using technology less.)

▶ *Reading and Writing 3, page 79*

Vocabulary Skill: Synonyms (15 minutes)

1. Have students read the information about synonyms.

2. Check comprehension by asking questions. *What is a synonym? Why should you learn synonyms? What do you have to be careful of when choosing synonyms?*

Skill Note

Many words that have similar meanings are not used in exactly the same contexts because they may differ in degree, in level of formality, in positive/negative connotation, or in how general or specific they are. A learners' thesaurus (such as the *Oxford Learner's Thesaurus*) can be useful for high-level students and for the teacher in helping to distinguish or explain the differences among similar words.

Tip for Success (5 minutes)

1. Read the tip aloud.

2. Write a sentence on the board that includes a word you could replace with a synonym. For example, *I was <u>surprised</u> when I found out my father is a Second Life user.*

3. Show students the entry for the word in a thesaurus, particularly a learner's thesaurus if you have one. Highlight the subtle differences in the meanings of the synonyms listed. Decide together which synonym would be the best one to replace the word in the sentence.

A (15 minutes)

1. Direct students to read the words in the box and work individually to rewrite the sentences.

2. Call on volunteers to read the completed sentences aloud.

> **Activity A Answers, p. 79**
> **2.** realistic;   **3.** limitations;   **4.** rare;
> **5.** experiments;   **6.** eventually, benefits

▶ *Reading and Writing 3, page 80*

B (10 minutes)

1. Read the directions and the two example sentences aloud. Explain that opportunities come in many forms, e.g., people could be given time or money or three chances to build a dream house, and all of those could be considered opportunities. *Freedom*, however, is a more specific kind of opportunity in this context.

2. Have students work individually to complete the activity. Elicit and discuss the answers.

> **Activity B Answers, p. 80**
> **2. a.** S, **b.** G;
> **3. a.** G, **b.** S;
> **4. a.** S, **b.** G;
> **5. a.** S, **b.** G

C (20 minutes)

1. Elicit the pairs of synonyms from Activities A and B. Tell students to choose five of the pairs to write their sentences.

2. Have students work with a partner to write their sentences. Monitor and provide feedback.

3. Ask volunteers to write pairs of sentences on the board. Correct as a class, focusing on the use of the synonyms rather than on grammatical issues.

 For additional practice with synonyms, have students visit *Q Online Practice*.

MULTILEVEL OPTION

Group lower-level students and work with this group. Choose pairs of synonyms and elicit sample sentences from the group orally. Allow everyone in the group to write the same sentences.

Activity C Answers, p. 80
Answers will vary. Ensure students have used the synonyms correctly.

▶ *Reading and Writing 3, page 81*

WRITING

21ST CENTURY SKILLS

In writing a summary, a person must identify the most important ideas in a piece of information and then present these ideas in a clear, concise form. This skill is invaluable for people in many different roles outside of the classroom: employees who need to give a debrief of events at a meeting, supervisors who need to report on the latest sales event, and community members who need to synthesize news information in order to make informed voting choices. After you have gone through the introduction to summarizing, discuss with students the various ways that they will make use of this skill in their lives.

Writing Skill: Writing a summary
(20 minutes)

1. Direct students to read the information about writing a summary.

---

2. Check comprehension: *Should a summary include sentences copied from the original? Should a summary include the main ideas? Should a summary include lots of examples? How long should a summary be? Should it include your opinions?*

A (5 minutes)

1. Direct students to read the summaries of Reading 1 and complete the activity individually.

2. Have students compare their answers with a partner and discuss which summary is more effective.

3. Call on volunteers to share their ideas with the class. Discuss why Summary A is not a good summary of Reading 1.

Activity A Answers, pp. 81–82
(checked):
1. Summary A, Summary B; **2.** Summary B;
3. Summary B; **4.** Summary B;
5. Summary A, Summary B; **6.** Summary B;
7. Summary B; **8.** Summary B

▶ *Reading and Writing 3, page 82*

B (5 minutes)

1. Direct students to read the sentences and check the ones that best summarize the ideas in Reading 2.

2. Ask students to compare their answers with a partner. Discuss why the other sentences do not summarize the ideas in Reading 2.

Activity B Answers, pp. 82–83
(checked): 1, 2, 5, 7, 8, 9

▶ *Reading and Writing 3, page 83*

C (10 minutes)

1. Elicit the topic sentence from Activity B. (Sentence number 2) Ask students to use the sentences from Activity B to write a summary of Reading 1.

2. Call on a volunteer to read the completed summary aloud.

Activity C Answers, p. 83
Sentences written out in this order: 2, 7, 5, 1, 9, 8

 For additional practice with summarizing, have students visit *Q Online Practice*.

Grammar: Parallel structure (10 minutes)

1. Read the information about parallel structure and go over the example sentences.

2. Check comprehension by writing unfinished sentences on the board: *I like to talk on my cell phone, play games on my computer, and ____; He didn't have a TV or ____.* Elicit a variety of parallel completions for each sentence.

Skill Note

Parallel structure often falls apart in students' writing when they try to connect longer or more complicated clauses and phrases (e.g., *He liked to talk on the phone, play computer games, and played soccer.*). Watch for these errors and copy them on the board to practice error correction with the class.

A (10 minutes)

1. Ask students to read the directions and work individually to complete the activity.

2. Elicit the answers from volunteers.

> **Activity A Answers, pp. 83–84**
> **2.** fly, meet, or build;
> **3.** realistic, but virtual;
> **4.** long walks, barbecues, and reruns;
> **5.** too tired, but not too tired;
> **6.** channel-surfing, and watching

▶ *Reading and Writing 3, page 84*

B (10 minutes)

1. Read the directions. Highlight the words in example number 1 that are repetitive and left out of the rewritten sentences (*They were*). Have students work with a partner to complete the activity.

2. Call on volunteers to write the combined sentences on the board. Ask them to name the parts of speech in the parallel structure and identify the conjunction used. Check punctuation as well as parallel structure.

> **Activity B Answers, p. 84**
> **2.** I didn't know what was on TV, but I didn't care.
> **3.** People should watch TV with moderation and a critical eye.
> **4.** Today's online environments are more complex, realistic, and exciting.
> **5.** Some people decide to be a fictional creature or a favorite comic-book character.
> **6.** They can forget about their first life and live through their second life.

Critical Thinking Tip (5 minutes)

1. Have a student read the tip aloud. Explain: *We often have to combine information from different sources when we are trying to learn about something, or when we want to make a point about something.*

2. Ask: *In what situations is it important to be able to combine information from different sources? For example, if you are writing a paper for a history class, why is it important to be able to combine information from a variety of sources? How is it important when you are trying to make a decision between two candidates during an election?*

Critical Q: Expansion Activity

Synthesize Information

Tell students that their two main sources of information in this unit are Readings 1 and 2. Ask them how they could combine ideas from the two readings. Use questions to guide them if necessary. Elicit and review the main ideas of Readings 1 and 2, discussing how the ideas could be combined. For example, the article about Second Life discusses a positive side of technology while the one about TV looks at a negative side. These ideas could be combined by contrasting how one uses the two kinds of technology: joining the website Second Life requires active participation while watching a TV show demands no activity and is completely passive. Or information from the two readings could be compared: the improvements the author of Reading 2 experienced—reading, sleeping and visiting friends more—could also be experienced by someone who avoided spending a lot of time online.

Q Unit Assignment: Write a summary and personal response

Unit Question (5 minutes)

Refer students back to the lists they made at the beginning of the unit about the advantages and disadvantages of technology. Tell them they can use the ideas to help them write their Unit Assignment paragraphs. Cue students if necessary by asking specific questions about the content of the unit: *What were some of the advantages and disadvantages of technology we discussed? How did the author's life change when she gave up TV?*

Learning Outcome

1. Tie the Unit Assignment to the unit learning outcome. Say: *The outcome for this unit is to write a summary and an opinion paragraph. This Unit Assignment is going to let you show your skills in summarizing, using synonyms, and using parallel structure.*

2. Explain that you are going to use a rubric similar to their Self-Assessment checklist on page 86 to grade their Unit Assignment. You can also share a copy of the Unit Assignment Rubric (on p. 44 of this *Teacher's Handbook*) with the students.

▶ *Reading and Writing 3, page 85*

Tip for Success (2 minutes)

1. Read the tip aloud.

2. Explain: *When you read a text, think about the six Wh- questions as you read. Answering these questions will help you identify the main ideas in the text.*

3. Elicit answers to the six *Wh-* questions for Reading 2.

Plan and Write

Brainstorm

A (15 minutes)

1. Ask students to work individually to write the main idea of the article and the details they remember. Tell them they should write from memory, without referring back to the article. This will help them write ideas from the article without plagiarizing or copying the words directly.

2. Have students read the instructions. Emphasize that the purpose of the questions is to guide their writing; they should not simply provide answers.

Plan

B (15 minutes)

1. Elicit a sample topic sentence for the summary of Reading 2. Then elicit any details the students wrote about the reading in Activity A. Write them on the board and discuss which details are irrelevant because they don't support the topic sentence. Cross these details out. Then direct students to read and follow the directions in number 1.

2. Have students work individually to complete the outlining tasks in numbers 2, 3, and 4. Monitor and provide feedback.

▶ *Reading and Writing 3, page 86*

Write

C (15 minutes)

1. Direct students to look at the Self-Assessment checklist on p. 86. Remind them that you will be using a similar rubric to evaluate their writing.

2. Ask students to work individually to write their paragraphs.

Alternative Unit Assignments

Assign or have students choose one of these assignments to do instead of, or in addition to, the Unit Assignment.

1. What technology (besides TV) do you use the most (for example, a cell phone or the Internet)? Do you think you could give it up for six months? For a year? Forever? Explain.

2. Using the Internet, find an article about another way people use technology in their free time, such as playing video games or listening to music online. Write a one-paragraph summary of the article.

 For an additional Unit Assignment, have students visit *Q Online Practice*.

Revise and Edit

Peer Review

A (15 minutes)

1. Pair students and direct them to read each other's work

2. Ask students to answer the questions and discuss them.

3. Give students suggestions for how to give helpful feedback: *I'm not sure this detail is necessary in the summary.*

Rewrite

B (10 minutes)

Students should review their partners' answers from A and rewrite their paragraphs accordingly.

Edit

C (10 minutes)

1. Direct students to read and complete the Self-Assessment checklist. They should be prepared to hand in their work or discuss it in class.

2. Ask for a show of hands for how many students gave all or mostly *yes* answers.

3. Use the Unit Assignment Rubric on p. 44 in this *Teacher's Handbook* to score each student's assignment.

4. Alternatively, divide the class into large groups and have students read their paragraphs to their group. Pass out copies of the Unit Assignment Rubric and have students grade each other.

▶ *Reading and Writing 3, page 87*

Track Your Success (5 minutes)

1. Have students circle the words they have learned in this unit. Suggest that students go back through the unit to review any words they have forgotten.

2. Have students check the skills they have mastered. If students need more practice to feel confident about the proficiency in a skill, point out the page numbers and encourage them to review.

3. Read the Learning Outcome aloud. Ask students if they feel that they have met the outcome.

Unit 4   New Perspectives

Unit Assignment Rubric

Student name: _____

Date: _____

Unit Assignment: *Write a summary and personal response.*

20 points = Paragraph element was completely successful (at least 90% of the time).
15 points = Paragraph element was mostly successful (at least 70% of the time).
10 points = Paragraph element was partially successful (at least 50% of the time).
 0 points = Paragraph element was not successful.

Summary and Personal Response	20 points	15 points	10 points	0 points
Student used correct punctuation and spelling.				
Paragraphs include vocabulary from the unit and a variety of synonyms.				
The summary includes the main ideas of the reading.				
Student clearly expressed an opinion in their paragraph and provided reasons and examples to support it.				
Parallel structures are used correctly.				

Total points: _____

Comments:

Unit QUESTION

Why do people help each other?

Responsibility

READING • using a graphic organizer
VOCABULARY • phrasal verbs
WRITING • stating reasons and giving examples
GRAMMAR • gerunds and infinitives

LEARNING OUTCOME

Write a paragraph about why people help others using reasons and examples.

▶ *Reading and Writing 3, pages 88–89*

Preview the Unit

Learning Outcome

1. Ask for a volunteer to read the unit skills, then the unit learning outcome.

2. Explain: *This is what you are expected to be able to do by the unit's end. The learning outcome explains how you are going to be evaluated. With this outcome in mind, you should focus on learning these skills (Reading, Vocabulary, Writing, Grammar) that will support your goal of writing a paragraph with reasons and examples. This can also help you act as mentors in the classroom to help the other students meet this outcome.*

A (15 minutes)

1. To get students thinking about the topic, ask: *What are some things people do to help each other? When do people need help?*

2. Put students in pairs or small groups to discuss the first two questions. Explain what *human nature* means.

3. Call on volunteers to share their ideas with the class. Ask follow-up questions: *What did you do to help someone recently? Do you know people who are always helping others?*

4. Focus students' attention on the photo. Have a volunteer describe the photo to the class. Read the question aloud. Ask if the man looks like he enjoys helping people.

Activity A Answers, p. 89
Answers will vary. Possible answers:

1. Yes. I think it's something we learn from our families./No, I think humans have a natural desire to help.

2. You shouldn't help someone if helping that person will hurt others or yourself. You shouldn't help someone who needs to learn how to help themselves (like a child in some situations).

3. The man is giving directions to a tourist.

B (20 minutes)

1. Introduce the Unit Question, *Why do people help each other?* Ask students if they think that people help each other because it is something they learned to do or because it is human nature. Give students a minute to silently consider their answers to the question. Have students who think helping behavior is mostly learned stand on one side of the room. Students who think helping behavior is mostly human nature should stand on the other side of the room.

2. Direct students to tell a partner next to them their reasons for choosing the answer they did.

3. Call on volunteers from each side to share their opinions with the class.

4. After students have shared their opinions, provide an opportunity for anyone who would like to change sides to do so.

5. Ask students to sit down, copy the Unit Question, and make a note of their answer and their reasons. They will refer back to these notes at the end of the unit.

Activity B Answers, p. 89
Answers will vary. Possible answers:
Lower-level answers: Your parents teach you to help. It feels good. It's natural.
Mid-level answers: When you help others, you feel like a better person. When you are young, you learn that helping is the right thing to do.
Higher-level answers: (Students may be able to supply examples to support their opinions.) I think people help each other because they are taught that helping is good, and they want to be helped themselves. For example, we help the elderly because we hope others will help us when we're older.

The Q Classroom (5 minutes)

⏵) CD 2, Track 2

1. Play The Q Classroom. Use the example from the audio to help students continue the conversation. Ask: *How did the students answer the question? Do you agree or disagree with their ideas? Why?*

2. Ask students to look over the ideas they wrote for Activity B. Give them time to add new ideas to their notes.

▶ *Reading and Writing 3, page 90*

C (5 minutes)

1. Ask students to read the questions and reflect on their answers.

2. Seat students in small groups and assign roles: a group leader to make sure everyone contributes, a note-taker to record the group's ideas, a reporter to share the group's ideas with the class, and a timekeeper to watch the clock.

3. Give students five minutes to discuss the questions. Call time if conversations are winding down. Allow them an extra minute or two if necessary.

4. Call on each group's reporter to share ideas with the class.

Activity C Answers, p. 90
Answers will vary. Possible answers:
1. When I'm sick; when I'm lost; when I don't know how to do something;
2. When they're poor, homeless, or hungry; during disasters;
3. Yes, because no one wants to be homeless./No, because I don't trust them to spend the money well. Yes, because I like to show people my city./No, because I'm shy, so I don't help people unless they ask. Yes, because I like children./Maybe not, if the child's parents are nearby to help.

D (10 minutes)

1. Direct students to look at the pictures. Have them continue working with their group from Activity C to answer the questions.

2. Elicit answers from various members of each group.

Activity D Answers, p. 90
Answers will vary. Possible answers:
1. (picture1) changing a flat tire, on the roadway; (picture 2) purse snatching, outside a bank or near an ATM; (picture 3) a man in wheelchair is being pushed across the street, in a crosswalk; (picture 4) people looking at map, on a roadway;
2. People help strangers because it's the right thing to do; because they would like to be helped if they were in these situations;
3. Yes. I have given tourists directions downtown.

EXPANSION ACTIVITY: Reasons Why (10 minutes)

1. Seat students in groups (or have them stay in their groups from Activities C and D) and give each group two pieces of poster paper. Tell them to title one paper *Reasons Why* and the other *Reasons Why Not*.

2. Bring up each situation from Activities C and D on p. 90. Tell the groups to write the reasons why they would or wouldn't help on the correct paper. Post the reasons or keep them to refer to later in the unit.

▶ *Reading and Writing 3, page 91*

READING

READING 1: A Question of Numbers

VOCABULARY (15 minutes)

1. Direct students to read the words and definitions in the box. Answer any questions about meaning or provide examples of the words in context. Pronounce and have students repeat the words. Highlight the syllable in each word that receives primary stress.

2. Have students work with a partner to complete the sentences. Call on volunteers to read the completed sentences aloud.

3. Have the pairs read the sentences together.

Vocabulary Answers, pp. 91–92		
1. According to;	**2.** witness;	**3.** complex;
4. theory;	**5.** responsibility;	**6.** prove;
7. end up;	**8.** factors;	**9.** apply to

 For additional practice with the vocabulary, have students visit *Q Online Practice*.

▶ *Reading and Writing 3, page 92*

PREVIEW READING 1 (5 minutes)

1. Ask students to look at the photo and describe the situation. (It's crowded.)

2. Read the directions. Discuss the word *bystander*.

3. Tell students to check their prediction and ask them to look back at it when they've finished the article.

Preview Reading 1 Answer, p. 92
(checked): when he or she is alone

Reading 1 Background Note

In addition to the diffusion of responsibility, there are other reasons cited for the bystander effect. It is possible that in some situations, bystanders are influenced by the fact that other people are not reacting; that is, they think that since no one else is reacting, it must not be necessary to do anything. In addition, people may feel that they are not competent to help or that other bystanders are more qualified.

The bystander effect is of concern in the workplace and at institutions like universities because it means that some people will be unwilling to come forward to talk about unacceptable behaviors they see. Some organizations conduct "active bystander" training to help people become more aware of their responsibility to act.

▶ *Reading and Writing 3, page 93*

READ (20 minutes)

 CD 2, Track 3

1. Instruct students to read the article. Remind them to refer to the glossed words. Tell them to mark any unknown vocabulary but to continue reading. Ask them to set their pens down or look up when they've completed the article.

2. When most students have finished reading, elicit and discuss their vocabulary questions.

3. Play the audio and ask students to read along silently.

▶ *Reading and Writing 3, page 94*

MAIN IDEAS (10 minutes)

1. Ask students to read the statements and work individually to complete the activity. Ask them to underline the sentences in the article that support their choices.

2. Call on volunteers for the answers. Discuss why some answers are false.

Main Ideas Answers, p. 94
1. T; **2.** F; **3.** T; **4.** F; **5.** T

▶ *Reading and Writing 3, page 95*

DETAILS (10 minutes)

1. Direct students to read the statements and circle the best answer. Encourage them to circle the information in the article that helped them choose each answer.

2. Call on volunteers to read the completed statements aloud.

Details Answers, p. 95
1. c; **2.** c; **3.** b; **4.** a; **5.** b

 For additional practice with reading comprehension, have students visit *Q Online Practice*.

ⓠ WHAT DO YOU THINK? (20 minutes)

1. Ask students to read the questions and reflect on their answers.

2. Seat the students in small groups and assign roles: a group leader to make sure everyone contributes, a note-taker to record the group's ideas, a reporter to share the group's ideas with the class, and a timekeeper to watch the clock.

3. Give students five minutes to discuss the questions. Call time if conversations are winding down. Allow them an extra minute or two if necessary.

4. Call on each group's reporter to share ideas with the class.

5. Have each student choose one of the questions and write five to eight sentences in response.

6. Call on volunteers to share their responses with the class.

MULTILEVEL OPTION

Seat students in mixed-ability groups so that lower-level students can benefit from listening to higher-level students.

Allow lower-level students to write three sentences in response to the question they choose.

Ask higher-level students to write responses to more than one question.

What Do You Think? Answers, p. 96

Answers will vary. Possible answers:

1. Yes, I once didn't help someone who needed help. I didn't help him because I was afraid of getting hurt. People might not help a stranger because they're afraid or because they don't think the stranger deserves it. They also might not help a stranger if they are in a hurry. They might think someone else who is not in a hurry can help the stranger.

2. I think people in cities are more helpful to strangers because they're more used to strangers. People in cities are surrounded by strangers all the time. They probably have had many experiences when strangers heve helped them. Also, people in cities probably see a lot of tourists who need help. It's easy to help tourists by giving them directions.

3. No, I don't think culture is a factor because helping others is human nature. I think anyone from any culture would want to help someone. For example, once I witnessed a car accident. The drivers were badly injured. Four other witnesses and I stopped our cars to help the injured drivers. We were from different cultures, but we all wanted to help.

Learning Outcome

Use the learning outcome to frame the purpose and relevance of Reading 1. Ask: *What did you learn from Reading 1 that will help you write a paragraph about why people help each other?* (Students learned about factors that make people hesitate to help others. They may want to use this information when they write their paragraphs.)

Reading Skill: Using a graphic organizer (5 minutes)

1. Direct students to read the information about graphic organizers and to study the diagram.

2. Check comprehension by asking questions: *How are graphic organizers useful? What does the example flow chart show?*

Tip for Success (2 minutes)

1. Read the tip aloud.

2. Explain to students that they can use a graphic organizer to organize information from a text.

3. Point out how the example graphic organizer organizes the information from Reading 1. Ask, *When do you think you might need to look for patterns of organization in a text?*

A (15 minutes)

1. Have students look at the organizer for paragraph 4 and discuss the questions with a partner.

2. Call on volunteers to share their responses with the class.

> **Reading Skill A Answers, p. 97**
> 1. It puts the information into groups: Research, Results, and Conclusion;
> 2. From the student;
> 3. Yes, because it puts similar information together and includes only the important information.

Critical Thinking Tip (5 minutes)

1. Have a student read the tip aloud. Explain: Making illustrations can make it easier to understand information or ideas.

2. Ask: *In your everyday life, when is it helpful to illustrate information or ideas? For example, if you are giving someone directions, how can you use an illustration? How can you use an illustration to organize your day or your month?*

Critical Q: Expansion Activity

Organize Information

Ask students if they find it easier to remember information when it is presented in a visual form. Point out that the thinking they do to create a visual representation helps them absorb the information.

Ask students to flip through the book and look for different graphic organizers. Then have them discuss how each one organizes information. For example, on p. 13, there is a T-chart that organizes information into two categories. There are also numerous charts that put information into more than two categories. On p. 48, there is an idea map that shows connections between ideas. On p. 186, a timeline shows information in chronological order. On p. 195, there is a chart that shows causes and effects. There are also many outlines that show the structure of an essay or paragraph. Ask if students are familiar with any other graphic organizers (such as Venn diagrams for comparison or organizational charts for showing hierarchies).

B (5 minutes)

1. Ask students to work with a partner to complete the summary of paragraph 4.

2. Go over the answers with the class.

> **Reading Skill B Answers, p. 97**
> **1.** three; **2.** alone; **3.** 62%; **4.** four;
> **5.** having more witnesses means people are less likely to help

 For additional practice with graphic organizers, have students visit *Q Online Practice*.

▶ *Reading and Writing 3, page 98*
READING 2: The Biology of Altruism

VOCABULARY (15 minutes)

1. Direct students to read the sentences and circle the answer choice that is closest to the bold word. Tell them to underline the context clues in each sentence that help them find the correct answer.

2. Put students in pairs to compare answers. Elicit the answers from volunteers. Have students repeat the bold vocabulary words. Highlight the syllable in each word that receives primary stress. Discuss the context clues.

3. Ask questions to help students connect with the vocabulary: *Who is the most **altruistic** person you know? Would you like to be a **subject** in a study like the one in Reading 1? What is something so small you can **barely** see it?*

> **Vocabulary Answers, pp. 98–99**
> **1.** b; **2.** b; **3.** a; **4.** b; **5.** c;
> **6.** a; **7.** a; **8.** b; **9.** b

 For additional practice with the vocabulary, have students visit *Q Online Practice*.

▶ *Reading and Writing 3, page 99*
PREVIEW READING 2 (5 minutes)

1. Have students read the directions. Then they should read the first and last paragraph of the article and check their predictions.

2. Tell students to review their predictions after reading.

> **Preview Reading 2 Answer, p. 99**
> (checked): It makes them feel good. It helps people survive.

▶ *Reading and Writing 3, page 100*
Reading 2 Background Note

Altruism is of great interest to biologists, who are trying to explain what advantages individuals and groups can gain from altruistic behavior. In addition to the neurological studies, further evidence for the biological basis of altruism comes from observations of animals. Altruistic behavior has been observed in a wide variety of animals, including vampire bats that share food and chimpanzees that adopt orphans.

READ (20 minutes)

 CD 2, Track 4

1. Instruct students to read the article and refer to the glossed words. Tell them to mark any unknown vocabulary but to continue reading. Ask them to set their pens down or look up when they've completed the article.

2. When most students have finished reading, elicit and discuss their vocabulary questions.

3. Play the audio and ask students to read along silently.

MAIN IDEAS (10 minutes)

1. Ask students to read and complete the activity individually. Students should find the information in the article that supports their answers.

2. Elicit the answers from the class.

> **Main Ideas Answers, p. 102**
> **1.** a; **2.** c; **3.** a; **4.** a; **5.** b

DETAILS (10 minutes)

1. Direct students to read the statements and complete the activity individually. Encourage them to underline sentences or phrases in the text that support their answers.

2. Go over the answers with the class. Elicit corrections for the false sentences.

> **Details Answers, p. 102–103**
> **1.** F ~~throw~~ drop;
> **2.** T;
> **3.** T;
> **4.** F ~~have known about mirror neurons for hundreds of years~~ have recently discovered mirror neurons;
> **5.** T;
> **6.** F ~~$1000~~ $100;
> **7.** F ~~memory~~ pleasure

 For additional practice with reading comprehension, have students visit *Q Online Practice*.

Ⓠ WHAT DO YOU THINK?

A (15 minutes)

1. Ask students to read the questions and reflect on their answers.

2. Seat students in small groups and assign roles: a group leader to make sure everyone contributes, a note-taker to record the group's ideas, a reporter to share the group's ideas with the class, and a timekeeper to watch the clock.

3. Give students five minutes to discuss the questions. Call time if conversations are winding down. Allow them an extra minute or two if necessary.

4. Call on each group's reporter to share ideas with the class.

Activity A Answers, p. 103
Answers will vary. Possible answers:
1. I'm very altruistic. I regularly spend part of my weekends serving food at the homeless shelter./I'm not that altruistic. I usually help my friends and family, but I don't help strangers very often.
2. I think some people were raised to value helping others more./I think the difference is biological.

B (5 minutes)

1. Tell the students that they should think about both Reading 1 and Reading 2 as they answer the questions in B. Students will choose one of the questions and write five to eight sentences in response.

2. Ask students to read their sentences with a partner.

3. Call on each pair to share their responses with the class.

Activity B Answers, p. 103
Answers will vary. Possible answers:
1. Our human nature makes us want to help others. Even babies want to help people. However, when other people are there, we might go against our nature. We might not help someone because we think someone else will help. Or we might think it's not necessary to help because no one else is helping.
2. Yes, because people who have been helped will want to help others. For example, my father had a very difficult childhood, but he was helped by a lot of people. Now he always tries to help others. On the other hand, someone who has received a lot of help might become selfish. They might not think about helping others because they expect others to do things for them all the time.

Learning Outcome

Use the learning outcome to frame the purpose and relevance of Readings 1 and 2. Ask: *What did you learn from Readings 1 and 2 that will help you write about why people help each other?* (In Reading 2, students learned that people seem to have a biological desire to help. However, they also learned that people might hesitate to help in situations where there are others around. Students may want to refer to this information in their Unit Assignment paragraphs.)

Vocabulary Skill: Phrasal verbs (5 minutes)

1. Direct students to read the information about phrasal verbs.

2. Check comprehension: *What is a phrasal verb? What's the difference in meaning between* end *and* end up? *What's the difference in meaning between* watch *and* watch out? *Elicit from students any other phrasal verbs that they know.*

Skill Note

Phrasal verbs are very common in both written and spoken English—there are well over 2,000 of them—so students might want a phrasal verb dictionary (such as *The Oxford Phrasal Verbs Dictionary for Learners of English*) for looking up these expressions. When learning new phrasal verbs, students should avoid trying to memorize lists of verbs with the same particle or the same base, as this is likely to result in confusion. Instead, phrasal verbs should be treated like other vocabulary items; students should make a note of the ones they come across in context and study their meaning and usage.

▶ *Reading and Writing 3, page 104*

A (15 minutes)

1. Direct students to work individually to match the phrasal verbs with their definitions. Encourage students to look back at the readings to ascertain the meaning of each phrasal verb.

2. Go over the answers with the class.

> **Activity A Answers, p. 104**
> **1.** d; **2.** f; **3.** c; **4.** e; **5.** a; **6.** b

B (10 minutes)

1. Direct students to complete the activity individually.

2. Call on volunteers for the answers.

> **Activity B Answers, p. 104**
> **1.** set up; **2.** figure out; **3.** point out;
> **4.** call out; **5.** grow out of; **6.** help out

MULTILEVEL OPTION

Seat lower-level students in small groups and allow them to help each other with Activities A and B. Monitor and assist these groups.

When higher-level students finish the activities, ask them to write original sentences using three of the phrasal verbs. Have volunteers write their sentences on the board and discuss them as a class, focusing on the use of the phrasal verbs rather than on other grammatical issues.

 For additional practice with phrasal verbs, have students visit *Q Online Practice*.

▶ *Reading and Writing 3, page 105*

WRITING

21ˢᵀ CENTURY SKILLS

Employers today are looking for workers who can express their ideas clearly by stating their opinions and giving solid reasons and examples to support them. Point out to students that this is a skill they will use throughout their lives. Elicit other situations where students might need to state an idea or opinion and support it with a reason and an example. (e.g., telling the restaurant manager that customers preferred the old brand of coffee: *This new one is bitter. Several people have complained to me.* Or telling a customer that the larger size of something makes more sense: *It's more economical. With this one, you save $1.25 by getting the larger size instead of two smaller sizes.*)

Writing Skill: Stating reasons and giving examples (20 minutes)

1. Read the information about stating reasons and giving examples in writing.

2. Check comprehension: *What does a reason explain? What is an example? Why do you need examples?*

3. Write: *Sometimes it's difficult to help a stranger* on the board. Elicit a reason and write it under the statement. Then elicit an example to go with the reason. Start the example with *For example*, or *For instance*. If you did the Expansion Activity on p. 46 of this *Teachers' Handbook*, take out the students' lists of reasons and elicit examples to back them up.

4. Read the information about stating reasons with *because*.

▶ *Reading and Writing 3, page 106*

Tip for Success (2 minutes)

1. Read the tip aloud.

2. After students have read the paragraphs in the box, elicit reasons using the given expressions. For example, *Explain why people might not help a stranded driver. Give another reason for why people may not want to help.*

A (5 minutes)

1. Direct students to read the paragraphs in the box. Then have partners work together to complete the activity.

2. Elicit the answers from the class. Then have students complete the outline.

> **Activity A Answers, p. 106**
> (checked): we might be too busy to help; (underlined): <u>people might not stop to help a stranded driver on the side of the road because they are in a hurry to get to work</u>; (checked): because they don't feel safe; (underlined): <u>when people hear a stranger scream in the middle of the night, they might be too scared to help out</u>; (checked): because we assume they can help themselves; (underlined): <u>if someone on the sidewalk seems to be lost, people think that he or she can find the necessary information without help.</u>
> **Outline: 1.** There are a number of reasons why someone might not help a stranger in need.
> **2. Reason 2:** People don't feel safe; **Example:** When people hear a stranger scream in the middle of the night, they might be too scared to help out.
> **2. Reason 3:** We assume people can help themselves; **Example:** If someone on the sidewalk seems to be lost, people think that he or she can find the necessary information without help. **3. Concluding sentence:** Time, safety, and thinking people can help themselves are just three of the many reasons a person chooses not to help others.

B (10 minutes)

1. Have students continue working with their partners from Activity A. Tell them to read the sentences, underline the reasons, and insert any missing commas.

2. Elicit the answers from volunteers. If necessary, project the sentences or copy them on the board so that students can see the comma placement.

> **Activity B Answers, pp. 106–107**
> **2.** <u>Because our brains have mirror neurons,</u>
> **3.** <u>because they wanted to prove their theory</u>
> **4.** <u>because many factors are involved</u>
> **5.** <u>because it improves their chances of survival</u>
> **6.** <u>Because the street was so busy,</u>

 For additional practice with stating reasons and giving examples, have students visit *Q Online Practice.*

▶ *Reading and Writing 3, page 107*

Grammar: Gerunds and infinitives
(10 minutes)

1. Read the information about forming gerunds and gerunds as subjects. Put a gerund on the board and elicit sentences that use it as a subject. For example, *Running _____. (feels good, is exhausting,* etc.)

2. Direct students to look at the verbs that are followed by gerunds. Elicit sentence completions for several of the verbs, e.g., *I always avoid _____* and *I need to practice _____.*

3. Direct students to look at the verbs that are followed by infinitives. Elicit sentence completions for some of the verbs, e.g., *I hope _____* and *I forgot _____.*

Skill Note

In some languages, it is not unusual for an infinitive to be the subject of a sentence. However, this usage is uncommon in English.

To help students learn which verbs are followed by gerunds and which verbs are followed by infinitives, identify the verbs that are frequently used or the ones that cause the most problems for students and conduct controlled practice. Start a sentence, *My friend and I discussed _____,* and go around the room, calling on various students to complete the sentence using a different gerund. To make this a game, write the sentence opener on the board and have teams come up with as many completions as possible. The team with the most (correct) completions in three minutes gets a point. Then move on to the next verb.

A (10 minutes)

1. Ask students to work individually to complete the sentences.

2. Call on volunteers to read the completed sentences aloud.

> **Activity A Answers, p. 107–108**
> **2.** Understanding human behavior;
> **3.** Helping other people;
> **4.** Donating money;
> **5.** Using brain scans;
> **6.** Living in a big city

B (10 minutes)

1. Ask students to work individually to complete the sentences.

2. Elicit the answers from the class.

> **Activity B Answers, p. 108**
> **2.** quit eating;
> **3.** considered moving;
> **4.** avoid buying;
> **5.** discuss writing;
> **6.** finished eating

C (10 minutes)

1. Have students work individually to complete the sentences.

2. Ask volunteers to write the answers on the board.

> **Activity C Answers, p. 108**
> **2.** to visit;
> **3.** speaking;
> **4.** to help;
> **5.** playing;
> **6.** swimming

 For additional practice with gerunds and infinitives, have students visit *Q Online Practice.*

Unit Assignment: Write a paragraph with reasons and examples

Unit Question (5 minutes)

Refer students back to the ideas they discussed at the beginning of the unit about why people help others (or not). Tell them they can use the ideas to help them write their Unit Assignment paragraph. Cue students if necessary by asking specific questions about the content of the unit: *What is the bystander effect? What did we learn about the biology of altruism?*

Learning Outcome

1. Tie the Unit Assignment to the unit learning outcome. Say: *The outcome for this unit is to write a paragraph about why people help others and provide reasons and examples. This Unit Assignment is also going to let you show your skill in using* because *to introduce reasons and in using phrasal verbs and gerunds correctly.*

2. Explain that you are going to use a rubric similar to their Self-Assessment checklist on p. 110 to grade their Unit Assignment. You can also share a copy of the Unit Assignment Rubric (on p. 55 of this *Teacher's Handbook*) with the students.

Plan and Write

Brainstorm

A (15 minutes)

Ask students to work with a group to brainstorm reasons that might affect a person's decision to help others. Students should write down their ideas.

Plan

B (15 minutes)

1. Review the function of a topic sentence and the difference between reasons and examples.

2. Have students work individually to complete their outlines. Monitor and provide feedback.

Write

C (15 minutes)

1. Read the writing directions aloud. Remind students that you are going to use a rubric similar to their Self-Assessment checklist on p. 110 to grade their Unit Assignment. Go over the checklist with the class.

2. Ask students to work individually to write their paragraphs.

Alternative Unit Assignments

Assign or have students choose one of these assignments to do instead of, or in addition to, the Unit Assignment.

1. Think about a specific time you helped a stranger. Write a paragraph that describes the situation and explains why you decided to help him or her.

2. Would you give money to a stranger who asked for it on the street? Why or why not? Write a paragraph with reasons and examples to explain your answer.

 For an additional Unit Assignment, have students visit *Q Online Practice.*

Revise and Edit

A (15 minutes)

1. Pair students and direct them to read each other's work

2. Ask students to answer the questions and discuss them.

3. Give students suggestions for how to give helpful feedback: *I like this reason. I think you need another example here. Can you explain why you think this?*

Rewrite

B (10 minutes)

Students should review their partners' answers from A and rewrite their paragraphs accordingly.

Edit

C (15 minutes)

1. Direct students to read and complete the Self-Assessment checklist. They should be prepared to hand in their work or discuss it in class.

2. Ask for a show of hands for how many students gave all or mostly *yes* answers.

3. Use the Unit Assignment Rubric on p. 55 in this *Teacher's Handbook* to score each student's assignment.

4. Alternatively, divide the class into large groups and have students read their paragraphs to their group. Pass out copies of the Unit Assignment Rubric and have students grade each other.

▶ *Reading and Writing 3, page 111*

Track Your Success (5 minutes)

1. Have students circle the words they have learned in this unit. Suggest that students go back through the unit to review any words they have forgotten.

2. Have students check the skills they have mastered. If students need more practice to feel confident about their proficiency in a skill, point out the page numbers and encourage them to review.

3. Read the Learning Outcome aloud. Ask students if they feel that they have met the outcome.

Unit 5   Responsibility

Unit Assignment Rubric

Student name: _____

Date: _____

Unit Assignment: *Write a paragraph about why people help others using reasons and examples.*

20 points = Paragraph element was completely successful (at least 90% of the time).
15 points = Paragraph element was mostly successful (at least 70% of the time).
10 points = Paragraph element was partially successful (at least 50% of the time).
 0 points = Paragraph element was not successful.

Paragraph with reasons and examples	20 points	15 points	10 points	0 points
Student wrote an organized paragraph explaining why people help others.				
The paragraph includes vocabulary from the unit.				
Student used *because* correctly to state reasons.				
Phrasal verbs are used correctly.				
Gerunds are used correctly as subjects and after verbs.				

Total points: _____

Comments:

READING • distinguishing facts from opinions	**LEARNING OUTCOME**
VOCABULARY • suffixes	
WRITING • writing a letter to the editor	Write a multiple-paragraph letter to
GRAMMAR • compound sentences	the editor expressing your opinion about advertising.

▶ *Reading and Writing 3, pages 112–113*

Preview the Unit

Learning Outcome

1. Ask for a volunteer to read the unit skills, then the unit learning outcome.

2. Explain: *This is what you are expected to be able to do by the unit's end. The learning outcome explains how you are going to be evaluated. With this outcome in mind, you should focus on learning these skills (Reading, Vocabulary, Writing, Grammar) that will support your goal of writing a letter to the editor expressing your opinion about advertising. This can also help you act as mentors in the classroom to help the other students meet this outcome.*

A (15 minutes)

1. Ask students to discuss ads that they have seen recently, ads they like, or ads that they don't like. What are the ads for? Do they think the ads are good or not? Ask them to name places where they see ads every day.

2. Put students in pairs or small groups to discuss the first two questions.

3. Call on volunteers to share their ideas with the class. Ask follow-up questions: *What are some things you would never buy based on an advertisement? Are there ads that you really like? Why do you like them?*

4. Focus students' attention on the photo. Have a volunteer describe the photo to the class. Read the question aloud. Discuss the ad.

Activity A Answers, p. 113
Answers will vary. Possible answers:
1. I tried a new soda because I heard it advertised on the radio a lot.

2. No, an ad has never helped me./Yes, just when I needed to see a doctor, I saw an ad at a bus shelter for a clinic.
3. They are next to a street. There was probably a hurricane or flood in the area.

B (20 minutes)

1. Read aloud the Unit Question, *Does advertising help or harm us?* Give students a minute to silently consider their answers to the question. Then ask students who would answer *help* to stand on one side of the room and students who would answer *harm* to stand on the other side of the room. (Tell students they need to make a choice—whichever answer they think is *most* true.)

2. Direct students to tell a partner next to them their reasons for choosing the answer they did.

3. Call on volunteers from each side to share their opinions and reasons with the class.

4. After students have shared their opinions, provide an opportunity for anyone who would like to change sides to do so.

5. Ask students to copy the Unit Question and make a note of their answer, or opinion, and reasons to support their opinion. They will refer back to these notes at the end of the unit.

Activity B Answers, p. 113
Answers will vary. Possible answers:
Lower-level: It harms us./It helps us.
Mid-level: It harms us because it makes us want things we don't need/It helps us because it provides us with useful information.
Higher-level: (Students may be able to provide anecdotes to back up their opinions.) I think advertising can be very helpful. If I hadn't seen the ad for this school, I would never have known to come here./I think it can be harmful. It makes us buy things we don't need, or things that are bad for us, like soda and fast food.

The Q Classroom (5 minutes)

CD 2, Track 5

1. Play The Q Classroom. Use the example from the audio to help students continue the conversation. Ask: *How did the students answer the question? Do you agree or disagree with their ideas? Why?*

2. Ask students to look over the notes they wrote for Activity B. Give them time to add any other ideas from the audio.

▶ *Reading and Writing 3, page 114*

C (5 minutes)

1. Seat students in small groups and have them discuss the questions.

2. Call on volunteers from each group to share ideas with the class. Discuss what each of the ads in the photos is selling and whether students think the ads are effective.

Activity C Answers, p. 114
Answers will vary. Possible answers:
1. in magazines, newspapers, stores, and stadiums; on television, the Internet, billboards, and vehicles
2. 1. on a highway; 2. on a city street; 3. in a town; 4. on a truck

D (10 minutes)

1. Read the directions. Ask students to work with their groups to fill out the chart.

2. Go over the answers as a class.

Activity D Answers, p. 114
Advertisement 1: to provide information, to provide help
Advertisement 2: to sell something
Advertisement 3: to provide information
Advertisement 4: to sell something

EXPANSION ACTIVITY: Effective Advertising (5 minutes)

Seat students in groups or have them continue working with their groups from Activities C and D. Give each group a magazine (or a few magazines) and ask them to pull out advertisements. Direct groups to answer these questions about the ads they choose.

Is the ad attractive? Why or why not?

Is the ad providing you with information or help, or is it selling you a product?

Does the ad give you useful information?

What message is the ad giving?

Do you think the ad is effective? Why or why not?
Ask the group to show their ads and share their answers with the class.

Critical Thinking Tip (5 minutes)

1. Have a student read the tip aloud. Explain: *We often put things into categories to help us organize them, and to more easily see the similarities and differences between the things.*

2. Ask: *In what situations do we have to think about how things are categorized? For example, if you're looking for a specific type of magazine, it's important to be able to look at a group of magazines and be able to understand how to categorize them. That way, if you want a health magazine, you won't accidentally buy a car magazine. You might categorize your CDs into the ones you listen to more often and the ones you listen to less often. How might you categorize your neighbors? Your classes? Your errands?*

Critical Q: Expansion Activity

Categorize Ads

For further practice with categorization, seat students in small groups and have them look for similarities and differences among magazine ads. (You can use the same ads from the previous Expansion Activity.)

Direct students to consider details such as the following: the way the people look, the amount of text in the ad, the way items appear or are photographed, and the words in the text. After they have categorized their ads, have each group present its findings to the class.

▶ *Reading and Writing 3, page 115*

READING

READING 1: Happiness Is in the Shoes You Wear

VOCABULARY (15 minutes)

1. Direct students to read the words and definitions in the box. Answer any questions about meaning or provide examples of the words in context. Ask students to complete the sentences with the words from the box.

2. Put students in pairs to compare answers. Elicit the answers from volunteers. Have

students identify the words or phrases in each sentence that give clues to the meaning of each vocabulary word.

3. Have students repeat the vocabulary words. Highlight the syllable in each word that receives primary stress.

MULTILEVEL OPTION

Group lower-level students and assist them with the task. Provide alternate example sentences or questions to help them understand the words. *What are the* **consequences** *if you don't study for a test? He said we should try a new restaurant; I think he's* **implying** *that he didn't like the last one. He doesn't want to study math, but he has to for his degree. Studying math is a* **means to an end.**

Have higher-level students complete the activity individually and then compare answers with a partner. Tell the pairs to write an additional sample sentence for each word or expression. Have volunteers write one of their sentences on the board. Correct the sentences with the whole class, focusing on the use of the vocabulary word or expression rather than other grammatical issues.

Vocabulary Answers, pp. 115–116
1. recent;
2. unpredictable;
3. relationship;
4. imply;
5. means to an end;
6. tune out;
7. trivial;
8. consequence;
9. possession

 For additional practice with the vocabulary, have students visit *Q Online Practice.*

▶ *Reading and Writing 3, page 116*
PREVIEW READING 1 (5 minutes)

1. Have students read the first sentence of each paragraph. Elicit what students think the author's opinion is.

2. Discuss any ads that try to make people believe the product will make them happy. If you did the Expansion Activity on p. 57 of this *Teacher's Handbook,* refer back to those ads when discussing the question.

Preview Reading Answers, p. 116
Answers will vary. Possible answers:
- The author's opinion is that it's wrong and that it leads people to think possessions are more important than relationships.
- Yes, I've seen ads like this. For example, there are many ads that show smiling, good-looking, healthy people using the product. One ad I saw showed a family driving in a van. They looked like they were having a wonderful time together.

▶ *Reading and Writing 3, page 117*
Reading 1 Background Note

Many people feel that they are not affected by advertising because, for the most part, the effects of advertising are slow and gradual. After repeated viewings of a product being presented in a certain way, people begin to develop an image of the product without even realizing where that image came from. For example, people may come to believe that a particular car is safe or that a certain shampoo makes your hair healthy and shiny. If students believe they are unaffected by advertising, name various well-known products and ask students to call out the impressions they have of the products. Then discuss where those impressions came from.

READ (20 minutes)

 CD 2, Track 6

1. Instruct students to read the article and remind them to refer to the glossed words. Tell them to mark any unknown vocabulary but to continue reading. Ask them to set their pens down or look up when they've completed the article.

2. When most students have finished reading, elicit and discuss their vocabulary questions.

3. Play the audio and ask students to read along silently.

▶ *Reading and Writing 3, page 118*
MAIN IDEAS (10 minutes)

1. Ask students to read the sentences and check the main ideas. Direct them to underline the sentences in the reading that tell them the main ideas.

2. Go over the answers with the class.

Main Ideas Answers, p. 118
(checked): 1, 2, 5

DETAILS (10 minutes)

1. Direct students to work individually to read the questions and label them *T* or *F*. Have students underline the information in the text that supports their answers.

2. Go over the answers with the class. Elicit corrections for each of the false statements.

> **Details Answers, p. 118**
> **1.** F ~~wealthy~~ loved;
> **2.** T;
> **3.** F ~~diamond necklace~~ phone system;
> **4.** T;
> **5.** F ~~pay close attention to ads and watch them closely~~ don't pay attention and tune them out;
> **6.** F ~~more~~ less

 For additional practice with reading comprehension, have students visit *Q Online Practice*.

▶ *Reading and Writing 3, page 119*

WHAT DO YOU THINK? (20 minutes)

1. Ask students to read the questions and reflect on their answers.

2. Seat students in small groups and assign roles: a group leader to make sure everyone contributes, a note-taker to record the group's ideas, a reporter to share the group's ideas with the class, and a timekeeper to watch the clock.

3. Give students five minutes to discuss the questions. Call time if conversations are winding down. Allow them an extra minute or two if necessary.

4. Call on each group's reporter to share ideas with the class.

5. Have each student choose one of the questions and write five to eight sentences in response.

6. Call on volunteers to share their responses with the class.

> **MULTILEVEL OPTION**
>
> Seat students in mixed-ability groups so that lower-level students can benefit from listening to higher-level students.
>
> Allow lower-level students to write three sentences in response to the question they choose.
>
> Ask higher-level students to write responses to more than one question.

What Do You Think? Answers, p. 119
Answers will vary. Possible answers:
1. Yes, things can make you happy. I received a camera that made me happy because it started my love for photography. If I didn't receive that camera, I wouldn't have discovered how much I loved photography. Now photography is my favorite hobby. I have been taking pictures for 12 years.
2. Yes, I bought a phone because of ads I saw for it. I liked all of the features described in the ads. I also liked the music in the ad. It was a cool song I had never heard before. It made me feel like the phone would make me cool like the song.

Learning Outcome

Use the learning outcome to frame the purpose and relevance of Reading 1. Ask: *What did you learn from Reading 1 that will help you write about whether advertising is helpful or harmful?* (Students read several arguments against advertising, which they may want to include in their letter to the editor.)

Reading Skill: Distinguishing facts from opinions (5 minutes)

1. Direct students to read the information about distinguishing facts from opinions.

2. Check comprehension by asking questions: *What is a fact? What is an opinion? What are some examples of words that express opinions?*

A (10 minutes)

1. Direct students to read the statements. Ask them to work individually to label the statements *F* or *O*.

2. Call on volunteers for the answers. Ask them to explain how they could prove each fact. Have them identify the words in the sentences that indicate an opinion.

> **Reading Skill A Answers, p. 119**
> **1.** O; **2.** F; **3.** O; **4.** F; **5.** O; **6.** O

▶ *Reading and Writing 3, page 120*

B (10 minutes)

1. Tell students to read each sentence and underline the words that make it an opinion.

2. Go over the answers with the class.

> **Reading Skill B Answers, p. 120**
> **1.** <u>always</u>; **2.** <u>silly</u>, <u>funny</u>, <u>nothing to worry about</u>;
> **3.** <u>favorite, beautiful</u>; **4.** <u>ridiculous</u>; **5.** <u>harmful</u>

For additional practice with distinguishing facts from opinions, have students visit *Q Online Practice*.

READING 2: In Defense of Advertising

VOCABULARY (15 minutes)

1. Direct students to read each sentence and guess what they think the bold word means. Then have them write the bold words next to the definitions.

2. Have students compare their answers with a partner.

3. Elicit the answers from volunteers. Have students identify context clues in each sentence. Model the pronunciation of the bold words, pointing out the syllable that receives primary stress.

> **Vocabulary Answers, pp. 120–121**
> **a.** annoying; **b.** annual; **c.** exposure;
> **d.** broadcasting; **e.** donations; **f.** entertain;
> **g.** support; **h.** surrounding; **i.** memorable

 For additional practice with the vocabulary, have students visit *Q Online Practice*.

▶ *Reading and Writing 3, page 121*
PREVIEW READING 2 (5 minutes)

1. Have students read the first and last paragraphs of the article and then talk about their answers to the question.

2. Tell students they should review their answers after reading.

> **Preview Reading 2 Answer, p. 121**
> Answers will vary. Possible answers:
> It provides jobs. It supports TV programming.

Reading 2 Background Note

The argument about whether advertising is benign or harmful has become more intense with the current practice of "personalized" advertising. Search engines on the Web can remember a user's previous searches and will bias search results toward them. For example, if you have searched for a particular product by brand name in the past, future search results that include that brand will be higher on your results list. In addition, social media sites use profile information to provide targeted advertising so that different users see different ads on their screens. Online retailers also keep purchase information and use it to make suggestions for further purchases. Some people see this personalized advertising as an invasion of privacy while others see it as a step toward making advertisements more useful to the consumer.

Culture note: The Super Bowl is an American football championship game played in the United States every year. It is extremely popular and is usually the most-watched American television broadcast of the year. Public broadcasting programs show mainly educational programming and are financed with public money.

READ (5 minutes)

🔊 CD 2, Track 7

1. Instruct students to read the article and remind them to refer to the glossed word. Tell them to mark any unknown vocabulary but to continue reading. Ask them to set their pens down or look up when they've completed the article.

2. When most students have finished reading, elicit and discuss their vocabulary questions.

3. Play the audio and ask students to read along silently.

▶ *Reading and Writing 3, page 123*
MAIN IDEAS (15 minutes)

1. Ask students to read the sentences and go back to the article to find where each main idea appears. Students should number the main ideas in the order that they appear in the reading.

2. Go over the answers with the class.

> **Main Ideas Answers, p. 123**
> **a.** 5, **b.** 3, **c.** 2, **d.** 1, **e.** 6, **f.** 4

DETAILS (10 minutes)

1. Direct students to write an example for each benefit listed in the chart.

2. Call on volunteers for the answers. Elicit several examples for each benefit.

> **Details Answers, p. 123**
> Answers will vary. Possible answers:
> *supports the arts:* pays for TV programs, including public broadcasting; brings audiences to movies; gives experience and exposure to performers;
> *helps support sports:* pays for fields, equipment, and athletes' salaries; draws viewers to the Superbowl;
> *PSAs:* provide information about diseases, medical problems, and public health and safety;
> *helps make the world more colorful:* provides work for clothing designers, photographers, models, artists, paper company workers, and store employees

For additional practice with reading comprehension, have students visit *Q Online Practice*.

WHAT DO YOU THINK?

A (15 minutes)

1. Ask students to read the questions and reflect on their answers.

2. Seat students in small groups and assign roles: a group leader to make sure everyone contributes, a note-taker to record the group's ideas, a reporter to share the group's ideas with the class, and a timekeeper to watch the clock.

3. Give students five minutes to discuss the questions. Call time if conversations are winding down. Allow them an extra minute or two if necessary.

4. Call on each group's reporter to share ideas with the class.

> **Activity A Answers, p. 123**
> Answers will vary. Possible answers:
> **1.** It means advertising isn't good, but we need it. I agree because businesses need to sell products for the economy to survive./I disagree because I don't think advertising is bad.
> **2.** Yes, I would. I don't like to see advertising./No, I'd rather see ads and pay lower prices.

▶ *Reading and Writing 3, page 124*

B (5 minutes)

1. Tell the students they should think about Reading 1 and Reading 2 as they answer the questions in Activity B. Students will choose one of the questions and write five to eight sentences in response.

2. Ask students to read their sentences with a partner.

3. Call on each pair to share their responses with the class.

> **Activity B Answers, p. 124**
> Answers will vary. Possible answers:
> **1.** I saw an ad recently for a car. The car was being driven along a road near the ocean. The driver and passenger were having a good time. They were laughing and singing. The ad had a positive effect on me because I thought that it would be fun to drive a nice car with friends along the coast of California.

2. I would like to see less advertising during sports events. You can't even watch a game without it being interrupted every five minutes. The constant interruption takes away from your enjoyment of it. You can miss things sometimes because of advertisements. When the ads are finished, you see an instant replay of what you missed. But that's not as exciting as seeing it live.

Learning Outcome

Use the learning outcome to frame the purpose and relevance of Readings 1 and 2. Ask: *What did you learn from Readings 1 and 2 that prepares you to write about whether advertising is harmful or helpful?* (Students learned a number of arguments both against and in favor of advertising that they may want to include in their letter to the editor.)

Vocabulary Skill: Suffixes (15 minutes)

1. Have students read the information about suffixes.

2. Check comprehension by asking students to define a suffix. Then elicit words they know with each of the endings from the chart.

3. Direct students to read the words and check the correct part of speech.

4. Call on volunteers for the answers. Elicit any other form of the word the students know.

> **Vocabulary Skill Answers, p. 124**
> (checked): **1.** adjective; **2.** noun; **3.** adverb; **4.** adjective; **5.** noun; **6.** adjective; **7.** noun; **8.** noun; **9.** adverb; **10.** adjective

Skill Note

Additional examples for each suffix:

-ful: graceful, hopeful, useful, peaceful

-able: acceptable, agreeable, chewable, uncontrollable

-ial: facial, industrial, racial, official

-er: smaller, larger, taller, wider

-ment: agreement, government, judgment, employment

-tion: relation, decoration, preparation, promotion

-ship: citizenship, leadership, membership, partnership

-ness: cleanliness, brightness, forgiveness, greatness

-ly: quickly, simply, confidently, colorfully

1. Read the tip aloud.

2. Explain: *When you read, pay attention to words with suffixes. This will help you with your reading comprehension. Suffixes provide clues to the part of speech and meaning of an unfamiliar word even if the exact meaning isn't clear.*

 For additional practice with suffixes, have students visit *Q Online Practice*.

▶ *Reading and Writing 3, page 125*

WRITING

21ST CENTURY SKILLS

Writing a letter to the editor can empower students because letters to the editor are a way for community members to express their opinions about local issues. Letter writing is also a skill that is very much desired by employers. An employee who knows how to express and support his or her opinion in writing is going to be highly valued. Although letters are usually sent electronically these days, a formal style is still required in business communication. Highlight the usefulness of letter writing by asking students to brainstorm various situations in which they might need to write a formal letter or email.

Writing Skill:
Writing a letter to the editor (10 minutes)

1. Direct students to read the information about writing a letter to the editor. Ask them if the newspapers in their countries have a *Letters to the Editor* section and if they ever read it. Discuss why people write letters to the editor.

2. Check comprehension: *What is a letter to the editor? What three sections does it have? What is the purpose of the introduction? the body? the concluding paragraph?*

A (5 minutes)

1. Direct students to read the letter to the editor.

2. Check comprehension. *What is the purpose of the letter?* (to express an opinion) *What reasons does the writer give for his or her opinion? How does the writer conclude the letter?*

▶ *Reading and Writing 3, page 126*

B (5 minutes)

1. Direct students to work individually to answer the questions.

2. Ask students to compare their answers with a partner.

3. Elicit the answers and discuss any variations with the class.

Activity B Answers, p. 126
1. (underlined): <u>I think product placement is horrible and should be banned from television;</u>
2. Reason: There is already too much advertising; Example: Huge billboards advertise products. You can see ads on buses, subways, trains, and taxicabs. You see ads before movies and on TV.
3. Reason: product placement is done without permission; Example: When product placement appears in the middle of the show, I can't just tune it out without turning off the entertainment;
4. (underlined): <u>That's why I think product placement should be banned from television before everything on television becomes one very long commercial;</u> before everything on television becomes one very long commercial

 For additional practice with writing a letter to the editor, have students visit *Q Online Practice*.

Tip for Success (3 minutes)

1. Read the tip aloud.

2. Elicit other greetings, such as *Dear Manager, Dear Mr. Burns,* and *To Whom it May Concern.*

3. Ask students to take note of the punctuation in the greeting and salutation. Make sure they know where they would sign the letter (below the closing salutation) if they were to send a printed copy.

▶ *Reading and Writing 3, page 127*
Grammar:
Compound sentences (10 minutes)

1. Read the information about compound sentences and review the examples.

2. Check comprehension by writing compound sentences without punctuation or conjunctions on the board: *He liked the new phone ____ he liked its price, too. He bought the phone ____ it wasn't that good after all. He was very unhappy with it*

_____ he returned it. He can trade it for a new phone _____ he can get his money back. Elicit the correct conjunction and the comma placement for each sentence.

Skill Note

Many students write run-on sentences and connect independent clauses with a comma rather than a conjunction. To help them practice identifying simple sentences that can be combined with conjunctions, seat students in groups and provide each group with sentence strips. Tell the groups to write compound sentences in their notebooks using the strips in any order and adding conjunctions where appropriate. Sample sentence strips: _She saw an ad for a book on the Internet; The book was cheap; She ordered the book; Her order never arrived; She called the company; No one answered the phone; Her credit card was charged; She was very annoyed. Finally, she spoke to a customer service representative; She can get a refund; She can re-order the book._

A (10 minutes)

1. Ask students to read the directions and work individually to complete the activity.

2. Elicit the answers from volunteers.

> **Activity A Answers, pp. 127–128**
> **2.** but, contrasting ideas;   **3.** so, result;
> **4.** but, contrasting ideas;   **5.** or, choice

▶ _Reading and Writing 3, page 128_

B (10 minutes)

1. Ask students to work individually to write the sentences. Then have them compare their sentences with a partner.

2. Call on volunteers to read their sentences aloud.

> **Activity B Answers, p. 128**
> **1.** I like to stay healthy, so I exercise every day.
> **2.** Sara Marcone is a very creative writer, and she has written five novels.
> **3.** The concert was entertaining, but it was a bit too long.
> **4.** We receive a lot of mail that advertises sales, but not everything in the store is on sale.
> **5.** She writes a humorous column in the newspaper, and I enjoy reading it every week.
> **6.** We can go out for dinner, or we can stay home.

C (10 minutes)

1. Have students write five compound sentences.

2. Ask volunteers to write their sentences on the board.

> **Activity C Answers, p. 128**
> Answers will vary. Ensure students have used conjunctions correctly, and have used each one at least once.

Q Unit Assignment:
Write a letter to the editor

Unit Question (5 minutes)

Refer students back to the ideas they discussed at the beginning of the unit about whether advertising helps or harms us. Tell them they can use the ideas to help them write their Unit Assignment letters. Cue students if necessary by asking specific questions about the content of the unit: _What were some examples given for how advertising harms people? What were some examples given for how advertising helps people?_

Learning Outcome

1. Tie the Unit Assignment to the unit learning outcome. Say: _The outcome for this unit is to write a letter to the editor expressing your opinion about advertising. This Unit Assignment is going to let you show your skill in writing a letter to the editor, using the vocabulary from the unit, and using suffixes and compound sentences._

2. Explain that you are going to use a rubric similar to their Self-Assessment checklist on p. 130 to grade their Unit Assignment. You can also share a copy of the Unit Assignment Rubric (on p. 65 of this _Teacher's Handbook)_ with the students.

▶ *Reading and Writing 3, page 129*

Plan and Write

Brainstorm

A (15 minutes)

Ask students to look back at the notes they wrote when they answered the Unit Question at the beginning of the unit. Have them list any additional reasons, examples, or ideas they've gathered from the readings in the unit. Tell them that at this stage they should write down every idea they have.

Plan

B (15 minutes)

1. Direct students to read through what they have written and circle their two best reasons and examples.

2. Have students work individually to complete their outlines. Monitor and provide feedback.

▶ *Reading and Writing 3, page 130*

Write

C (15 minutes)

1. Direct students to look at the Self-Assessment checklist on p. 130. Go over the items on the checklist. Remind them that you will be using a similar rubric to evaluate their writing.

2. Ask students to work individually to write their paragraphs.

Alternative Unit Assignments

Assign or have students choose one of these assignments to do instead of, or in addition to, the Unit Assignment.

1. Think of an advertisement that you dislike and write a letter to the company explaining why you think the ad is offensive or ineffective.

2. Choose an advertisement for a product that you like and write a paragraph describing the ad and its message. Explain why you think the message is effective.

 For additional Unit Assignment, have students visit *Q Online Practice.*

Revise and Edit

Peer Review

A (15 minutes)

1. Pair students and direct them to read each other's work

2. Ask students to answer the questions and discuss them.

3. Give students suggestions for how to give helpful feedback: *You have two good reasons, but this reason could use an example.*

Rewrite

B (10 minutes)

Students should review their partners' answers from A and rewrite their paragraphs accordingly.

Edit

C (10 minutes)

1. Direct students to read and complete the Self-Assessment checklist. They should be prepared to hand in their work or discuss it in class.

2. Ask for a show of hands for how many students gave all or mostly *yes* answers.

3. Use the Unit Assignment Rubric on p. 65 in this *Teacher's Handbook* to score each student's assignment.

4. Alternatively, divide the class into large groups and have students read their paragraphs to their group. Pass out copies of the Unit Assignment Rubric and have students grade each other.

▶ *Reading and Writing 3, page 131*

Track Your Success (5 minutes)

1. Have students circle the words they have learned in this unit. Suggest that students go back through the unit to review any words they have forgotten.

2. Have students check the skills they have mastered. If students need more practice to feel confident about their proficiency in a skill, point out the page numbers and encourage them to review.

3. Read the Learning Outcome aloud. Ask students if they feel that they have met the outcome.

Unit Assignment Rubric

Student name: _____

Date: _____

Unit Assignment: *Write a multiple-paragraph letter to the editor expressing your opinion about advertising.*

20 points = Letter element was completely successful (at least 90% of the time).
15 points = Letter element was mostly successful (at least 70% of the time).
10 points = Letter element was partially successful (at least 50% of the time).
 0 points = Letter element was not successful.

Letter to the Editor	20 points	15 points	10 points	0 points
Student clearly expressed an opinion about advertising.				
Letter includes vocabulary from the unit and words with suffixes.				
Letter includes an introductory paragraph that states an opinion and a concluding paragraph that restates the opinion.				
Letter includes two body paragraphs with reasons and examples.				
Student used compound sentences correctly.				

Total points: _____

Comments:

7

Unit QUESTION
Why do people take risks?

Risk

READING • using referents to understand contrast
VOCABULARY • using the dictionary
WRITING • writing a narrative essay
GRAMMAR • shifts between past and present

LEARNING OUTCOME

Develop a narrative essay describing a risk you have taken

▶ *Reading and Writing 3, pages 132–133*
Preview the Unit

Learning Outcome

1. Ask for a volunteer to read the unit skills, then the unit learning outcome.

2. Explain: *This is what you are expected to be able to do by the unit's end. The learning outcome explains how you are going to be evaluated. With this outcome in mind, you should focus on learning these skills (Reading, Vocabulary, Writing, Grammar) that will support your goal of writing a narrative essay about a time you took a risk. This can also help you act as mentors in the classroom to help the other students meet this outcome.*

A (15 minutes)

1. Discuss the first question with the class. Use the students' input to write a definition of *take a risk* on the board. Elicit several examples of risks and write them on the board. Discuss both big risks and small risks. Explain that you might call someone a "risk-taker" if they take risks.

2. Put students in pairs or small groups to discuss the second question.

3. Call on volunteers to share their ideas with the class. Ask follow-up questions: *Why do you like / not like to take risks? Do you think some people are born to be risk-takers?*

4. Focus students' attention on the photo. Have a volunteer describe the photo to the class. Ask if students are familiar with motocross (the extreme sport of off-road or obstacle-course motorcycle racing). Read the question aloud.

Activity A Answers, p. 133
Answers will vary. Possible answers:
1. to do something that might have a negative outcome;
2. Yes, I'm a risk-taker. I like extreme sports/No, I'm not a risk-taker. I'm always very careful.
3. He is taking a physical risk because he enjoys the speed of racing.

B (20 minutes)

1. Read the Unit Question aloud, *Why do people take risks?* Tell students, *Let's start off our discussion by listing risky things that people do.*

2. Seat students in small groups and direct them to pass around a piece of paper as quickly as they can, with each group member adding one example of risky behavior to the list. Tell them they have two minutes to make the lists and they should list as many things as possible.

3. Call time and ask a reporter from each group to read the list aloud.

4. Use items from the lists as a springboard for discussion. For example: *Which of these things do people do for fun? Which do they do because they have to? Are any of the listed items financial risks? Social risks? Emotional risks?*

Activity B Answers, p. 133
Answers will vary. Possible answers:
Lower-level: It's exciting. It's fun.
Mid-level: Taking risks makes you appreciate life; it raises your adrenaline levels; modern life is too safe– it doesn't provide enough excitement.
Higher-level: (Students may be able to support their opinions with examples.) People who take risks feel more alive when they're facing death. I saw a movie about a soldier whose job was to diffuse bombs. When he was at home, not risking his life, he felt like things were dull and pointless.

CD 2, Track 8

1. Play The Q Classroom. Use the example from the audio to help students continue the conversation. Ask: *How did the students answer the question? Do you agree or disagree with their ideas? Why?*

2. Ask students to look over the lists they made for Activity B. Give them time to add any ideas they liked from the audio.

▶ *Reading and Writing 3, page 134*

C (5 minutes)

1. Have students work individually to rank the activities by level of risk. Then have them compare answers with a partner.

2. Call on volunteers to share their answers. Ask students to explain their opinions. Survey the class to see if there is general agreement about the riskiest or least risky activity.

> **Activity C Answers, p. 134**
> Answers will vary.

D (10 minutes)

1. Have students work individually to rank the jobs by level of risk. Then have them compare answers with the same partner from Activity C.

2. Go over their ideas as a class. Discuss the risks involved with each activity. Discuss if there is any agreement on the most and least dangerous jobs.

> **Activity D Answers, p. 134**
> Answers will vary.

EXPANSION ACTIVITY:
Discussing Consequences (10 minutes)

Help students generate vocabulary that may be useful when they are describing the consequences of risky behavior. Seat them in small groups (or have them continue working with their groups from Activity C and D). Have half the groups look at Activity C and the other half look at Activity D. Tell them to list the various things that might go wrong in the pictured activities. Encourage students to get as specific as possible. Examples: fall, hit a tree, not be able to reach medical help, break a rope, crash, have a blowout, drown, lose an oar, etc.

▶ *Reading and Writing 3, page 135*

READING

READING 1: Fear Factor:
Success and Risk in Extreme Sports

VOCABULARY (15 minutes)

1. Direct students to read each sentence and try to guess what the bold word means. Then have them choose the answer that best matches the meaning of the bold word.

2. Put students in pairs to compare answers. Elicit the answers from volunteers. Have students repeat the vocabulary words.

> **Vocabulary Answers, pp. 135–136**
> **1.** a; **2.** a; **3.** a; **4.** b; **5.** b;
> **6.** b; **7.** a; **8.** a; **9.** a; **10.** a

 For additional practice with the vocabulary, have students visit *Q Online Practice*.

MULTILEVEL OPTION

Group lower-level students and assist them with the task. Provide alternate example sentences or questions to help them understand the words. *His main athletic **pursuits** are tennis and horseback riding. Do you know anyone with a high **tolerance** for pain? Einstein had many **notable** achievements in physics. One **trait** a nurse needs is patience.*

Have higher-level students complete the activity individually and then compare answers with a partner. Tell the pairs to write an additional sample sentence for each word. Have volunteers write one of their sentences on the board. Correct the sentences with the whole class, focusing on the use of the word rather than other grammatical issues.

▶ *Reading and Writing 3, page 136*

PREVIEW READING 1 (5 minutes)

1. Have students read the directions and the first sentence of each paragraph of the reading that starts on p. 137. Tell them to check their ideas about why people do things like extreme sports. Have them list any other reasons.

2. Tell them they should review their answers after reading.

Reading 1 Background Note

Which sports are classified as "extreme sports" varies somewhat from source to source. Although the term always refers to sports that have an element of risk and danger, it is more often used to describe youth-oriented sports such as snowboarding, BMX racing, and motocross. This is partly because of the popularity of the X-games, a winter and summer extreme sports competition that features youth-oriented sports.

Extreme sports athletes may be different from other people who take large risks because they are normally very focused on a goal, and they have a desire to outperform themselves, which is a major reason they continue to push themselves in their sports. Many of these athletes would say that their desire to reach higher and higher goals is greater than their desire for a quick adrenaline rush.

▶ *Reading and Writing 3, page 137*

READ (20 minutes)

 CD 2, Track 9

1. Instruct students to read the article and refer to the glossed words. Tell them to mark any unknown vocabulary but to continue reading. Ask them to set their pens down or look up when they've completed the article.

2. When most students have finished reading, elicit and discuss their vocabulary questions.

3. Play the audio and ask students to read along silently.

▶ *Reading and Writing 3, page 138*

MAIN IDEAS (10 minutes)

1. Ask students to read the sentences and number the main ideas. Have them underline the sentences in the reading that tell them the main idea for each paragraph.

2. Go over the answers with the class.

> **Main Ideas Answers, p. 138**
> **1.** 5; **2.** 4; **3.** 3; **4.** 2

▶ *Reading and Writing 3, page 139*

DETAILS (10 minutes)

1. Direct students to work individually to find the statements in the reading and complete them.

2. Elicit the answers from volunteers.

> **Details Answers, p. 139**
> **1.** the fun of it; **2.** mental character;
> **3.** could be killed; **4.** without oxygen;
> **5.** people think it is

 For additional practice with reading comprehension, have students visit *Q Online Practice.*

WHAT DO YOU THINK? (20 minutes)

1. Ask students to read the questions and reflect on their answers.

2. Seat students in small groups and assign roles: a group leader to make sure everyone contributes, a note-taker to record the group's ideas, a reporter to share the group's ideas with the class, and a timekeeper to watch the clock.

3. Give students five minutes to discuss the questions. Call time if conversations are winding down. Allow them an extra minute or two if necessary.

4. Call on each group's reporter to share ideas with the class.

5. Have each student choose one of the questions and write five to eight sentences in response.

6. Call on volunteers to share their responses with the class.

MULTILEVEL OPTION

Seat students in mixed-ability groups so that lower-level students can benefit from listening to higher-level students.

Allow lower-level students to write three sentences in response to the question they choose.

Ask higher-level students to write responses to more than one question.

What Do You Think? Answers, p. 139

Answers will vary. Possible answers:

1. I think downhill skiing is risky. You are moving incredibly fast, and you can easily fall and injure yourself. Also, if you do injure yourself, you're up in the mountains far from a hospital. Someone who skis frequently wouldn't see downhill skiing as that risky because they have probably skied many times without getting hurt. They probably feel very much in control when they ski.

2. Yes, fishing seems risky. The ocean is dangerous and unpredictable. If you have an accident on the ocean, there might not be anyone around to help you. You could die from the cold water, or you could drown. You could also be eaten by a shark.

3. Mountain climbing seems very dangerous to people who don't do it because they aren't familiar with the safety equipment and the skills that mountain climbers have. They imagine climbing without equiptment, and that would be scary and dangerous. And if you fell from a mountain, you would probably die. Also, accidents are big news stories. People hear more about climbers that have accidents than they do about climbers who don't have any problems.

Learning Outcome

Use the learning outcome to frame the purpose and relevance of Reading 1. Ask: *What did you learn from Reading 1 that will help you write about a risk you have taken?* (Students learned some ways to talk about their own perceptions of and attitudes towards risk.)

▶ *Reading and Writing 3, page 140*

Reading Skill: Using referents to understand contrast (5 minutes)

1. Direct students to read the information about referents.

2. Check comprehension by asking questions: *What is a referent? How does the writer refer to people who enjoy extreme sports? How does the writer refer to those who don't enjoy extreme sports?*

A (10 minutes)

1. Direct students to read the directions and work individually to complete the activity.

2. Call on volunteers for the answers.

Reading Skill A Answers, p. 140

1. some people, (the rest of us;)
2. (most of us) others;
3. (many people) others;
4. certain people, (others;)
5. these types of people, (others)

▶ *Reading and Writing 3, page 141*

B (10 minutes)

1. Tell students to read the directions and work individually to complete the activity.

2. Go over the answers with the class. Create a T-chart on the board listing the words used to refer to fishermen in one column and words used to refer to the majority of people in the other column.

Reading Skill B Answers, p. 141

(most of us,) (the majority of people,) some people, These types of people, them, (The rest of us,) a certain type of person, certain types of people, (the rest of us)

 For additional practice with using referents, have students visit *Q Online Practice.*

READING 2: The Climb of My Life

VOCABULARY (15 minutes)

1. Direct students to read the words and definitions in the box. Answer any questions about meaning or provide examples of the words in context. Pronounce and have students repeat the words. Highlight the syllable in each word that receives primary stress.

2. Have students work with a partner to complete the sentences. Call on volunteers to read the completed sentences aloud. Practice the pronunciation of the bold words.

Vocabulary Answers, pp. 141–142

1. goal;	**2.** conquer;	**3.** determined;
4. bravely;	**5.** role;	**6.** distinctive;
7. earn;	**8.** ultimate;	**9.** significant

 For additional practice with the vocabulary, have students visit *Q Online Practice.*

PREVIEW READING 2 (5 minutes)

1. Have students read the title and the first two paragraphs of the article. Then elicit their predictions about why Kelly Perkins took this risk.

2. Tell students they should review their predictions after reading.

> **Preview Reading 2 Answer, p. 142**
> She wanted to change her image. She didn't want to be seen or to see herself as a "patient" anymore.

Reading 2 Background Note

Since her climb of Half Dome, Kelly Perkins has climbed a number of other significant peaks, including Mt. Fuji in Japan, Kilimanjaro in Tanzania, and the Matterhorn in Switzerland. She also returned to Yosemite to climb El Capitan (a much steeper ascent than Half Dome), and did a very challenging free climb (using only hands and feet to climb rather than ropes) in the Andes. She has publicized her climbs in the hope that by showing that transplant patients can lead a full life, she will inspire people to become organ donors. Her husband has accompanied her on every climb and has given her a new gold charm on the completion of each one.

READ (5 minutes)

 CD 2, Track 10

1. Instruct students to read the article and refer to the glossed words as they read. Tell them to mark any unknown vocabulary but to continue reading. Ask them to set their pens down or look up when they've completed the article.

2. When most students have finished reading, elicit and discuss their vocabulary questions.

3. Play the audio and ask students to read along silently.

MAIN IDEAS (15 minutes)

1. Ask students to read the sentences. Have them go back to the article to find each main idea and underline it. Then students should number the main ideas in the order that they appear in the reading.

2. Go over the answers with the class.

> **Main Ideas Answers, p. 145**
> **a.** 3, **b.** 4, **c.** 2, **d.** 1, **e.** 6, **f.** 5

DETAILS (10 minutes)

1. Direct students to work individually to complete the statements. Have them identify the information in the article that helps them complete each sentence.

2. Elicit the answers from volunteers.

> **Details Answers, p. 145**
> **1.** 4,100; **2.** imperfect; **3.** 1996; **4.** 45;
> **5.** 500; **6.** the bracelet

 For additional practice with reading comprehension, have students visit *Q Online Practice*.

WHAT DO YOU THINK?

A (15 minutes)

1. Ask students to read the questions and reflect on their answers.

2. Seat students in small groups and assign roles: a group leader to make sure everyone contributes, a note-taker to record the group's ideas, a reporter to share the group's ideas with the class, and a timekeeper to watch the clock.

3. Give students five minutes to discuss the questions. Call time if conversations are winding down. Allow them an extra minute or two if necessary.

4. Call on each group's reporter to share ideas with the class.

> **Activity A Answers, p. 146**
> Answers will vary. Possible answers:
> **1.** She would rather face the challenge of climbing mountains than the challenge of being ill.
> **2.** Yes, because after her transplant she was trying to change her image and prove herself./No, because she always loved the challenge and loved being outdoors.

B (5 minutes)

1. Tell the students that they should think about both Reading 1 and Reading 2 as they discuss the questions in Activity B. Students will choose one of the questions and write five to eight sentences in response.

2. Ask students to read their sentences with a partner.

3. Call on volunteers to share their responses with the class.

Activity B Answers, p. 146
Answers will vary. Possible answers:
1. Yes. They need to take risks because they wouldn't be happy without the adrenaline rush. Life without risk would seem dull. I think they would be unhappy. If they didn't do risky sports, they might find riskier things to do. For example, they might drive too fast on the highway to get the adrenaline rush.
2. Yes, most people perceive risk differently when they are older. When you are young, the possibility of serious injury isn't very real. When you get older and have more experience, it becomes more real. I think that's because you have more life experience. When you're older, you've seen the things that can happen when you take risks.

Learning Outcome

Use the learning outcome to frame the purpose and relevance of Readings 1 and 2. Ask: *What did you learn from Readings 1 and 2 that prepares you to write about a risk you have taken?* (Students may have gotten ideas to help them write about why they took a specific risk and who supported them in taking it.)

Vocabulary Skill: Using the dictionary (5 minutes)

1. Have students read the information about finding the correct meaning.
2. Check comprehension by asking students about the example. *How many definitions does* consume *have? Which one is correct for this context? How do you know?*

▶ *Reading and Writing 3, page 147*

A (10 minutes)

1. Direct students to read the sentences and identify the correct definitions of the underlined words in their dictionaries. Then have them compare answers with a partner.
2. Call on volunteers for the answers. Discuss any disagreements.

Activity A Answers, p. 147
1. drive: to cause somebody to do something; embrace: to accept eagerly;
2. appetite: a strong desire;
3. ingredient: one of the items you need to make something (figurative);
4. role: the function or position that somebody has or is expected to have;
5. earned: got something you deserved;
6. face: the front or one side of something

B (15 minutes)

1. Direct students to work with a partner to write sentences with three of the words from Activity A. Tell them to use the same definition.
2. Ask volunteers to write one of their sentences on the board.

Activity B Answers, p. 147
Answers will vary. Possible answers: *My desire to learn English drove me to study in the U.S. I embrace new ideas. I don't have an appetite for risk.*

Skill Note

Students at this level should be working with an all-English learner's dictionary (such as the *Oxford Dictionary of American English for Learners*). If your students are still relying heavily on their bilingual dictionaries, encourage them to transition to using the bilingual dictionary as a backup and turning first to the learner's dictionary. Conduct periodic activities with the dictionary to encourage students to become familiar with it. For example, when new vocabulary words are assigned, ask them to look up the words and identify the correct definition if there is more than one. Have them use the dictionary to find word families, synonyms, and example sentences as well.

21ST CENTURY SKILLS

Employers place a premium on independent thinking and the ability to use resources. Teaching students how to use the dictionary helps them achieve learner independence and gives them access to a life-long resource. Point out to students that the process of looking up a word and choosing the right definition based on context is helping them become independent learners. To help students practice this skill, follow this procedure when they read in class: Have everyone mark any unknown vocabulary words and collect the list on the board. Assign different words to different students (or groups of students) and have them look up their assigned words, identify the correct definitions, and share the definitions with the class.

 For additional practice with finding the correct meaning, have students visit *Q Online Practice.*

WRITING

Writing Skill:
Writing a narrative essay (10 minutes)

1. Direct students to read the information about writing a narrative essay.

2. Check comprehension: *What is a narrative essay? What three sections does it have? What is the purpose of the introduction? the body paragraphs? the concluding statement?*

Tip for Success (1 minute)

1. Read the tip aloud.

2. Elicit situations in which students might need to describe something that happened in their lives (e.g., in an application for a school).

A (5 minutes)

1. Direct students to read the narrative essay. Explain that the essay is about Kelly Perkins's second climb.

2. Check comprehension. *What background does she give in the introductory paragraph? Where does she state her main idea? What events does she describe in the body paragraphs? What does she say in the concluding statement?*

B (5 minutes)

1. Direct students to work individually to answer the questions.

2. Ask students to compare their answers with a partner.

3. Elicit the answers and discuss any variations with the class.

> **Activity B Answers, p. 149**
> **1.** (The first paragraph should be checked.)
> **2.** A few months after the Half Dome climb, I decided to climb Mt. Whitney in California.
> **3.** One. (The second paragraph should be bracketed.)
> **4.** (underlined): <u>tallest mountain in the continental U.S., spectacular blue sky, final steps, geographical marker identifying the summit, highest point on the continental United States.</u>
> **5.** I had made it to the peak, this time with a second heart and my husband.

 For additional practice with writing a narrative essay, have students visit *Q Online Practice.*

Grammar: Shifts between past and present (10 minutes)

1. Read the information about shifts between past and present and go over the examples.

2. Check comprehension by asking questions: *Why do writers use simple past? past perfect? simple present?* Point to the sentence with the past perfect and ask which happened first, the writer wanting to do something or her family developing an image of her. Explain that the past perfect is used to show that one action happened earlier than another.

Skill Note

The past perfect can be difficult for students to grasp. To help them understand the concept, use timelines. For example, put a simple timeline on the board with:

5:00 Joe left a message

6:00 I got home

Then write sample sentences: *When I got home, Joe left a message. When I got home, Joe had left a message.* Ask students which is true according to the timeline.

A (10 minutes)

1. Ask students to read the directions and work individually to complete the activity. Then have them compare their answers with a partner.

2. Elicit the answers from volunteers.

> **Activity A Answers, p. 150**
> (underlined): decided, had wanted, were, looked, considered, took, wanted, gathered, rolled, knew, meant, had made, felt, raised, cried out, did; (circled): is, hike, manage

B (10 minutes)

1. Ask students to read the directions and complete the activity individually.

2. Call on volunteers for the answers.

> **Activity B Answers, p. 150**
> **2.** past/present
> **3.** present/present
> **4.** past/past
> **5.** present/past

C (10 minutes)

1. Direct students to work individually to complete the sentences.

2. Call on several volunteers to read their completions to the class in order to get a variety of answers.

Activity C Answers, p. 150
Possible answers:
2. I never drink soda;
3. I speak English well;
4. people wore traditional clothes every day;
5. I eat at home;
6. I read and do homework

▶ *Reading and Writing 3, page 151*

Q° **Unit Assignment:** Write a narrative essay

Critical Thinking Tip (5 minutes)

1. Have a student read the tip aloud. Explain: *Nearly every day, we have to report information. It's important to be able to report information in a way that our listeners or readers can clearly understand.*

2. Ask: *In your everyday life, when do you need to report information? For example, what kind of information might you need to report to the police? Your friends? Your teacher?*

Critical Q: Expansion Activity

Report an Event

Ask students what kinds of decisions they make when they report an event. (For example, how much of the story to tell, which details are or are not important, what is the best order to tell the story in, etc.)

To give students practice with reporting events, have them journal for ten minutes every day about something that happened that day. After a week or two, have students go through their journal entries and choose one for you to read. Suggest that they look it over and revise it before they turn it in to you.

Unit Question (5 minutes)

Refer students back to the ideas they discussed at the beginning of the unit about why people take risks. Tell them they can use the ideas to help them write their Unit Assignment narratives. Cue students if necessary by asking specific questions about the content of the unit: *Why do people do extreme sports? Why did Kelly Perkins climb Half Dome?*

Learning Outcome

1. Tie the Unit Assignment to the unit learning outcome. Say: *The outcome for this unit is to write a personal narrative about a risk you took. This Unit Assignment is going to let you show your skill in using the vocabulary from the unit, using time shifts, and writing a narrative essay.*

2. Explain that you are going to use a rubric similar to their Self-Assessment checklist on p. 152 to grade their Unit Assignment. You can also share a copy of the Unit Assignment Rubric (on p. 75 of this *Teacher's Handbook*) with the students.

Plan and Write

Brainstorm

A (15 minutes)

Have students work individually to list any risks they have taken. Tell them to write as many as they can think of. Ask any willing volunteers to read aloud some items from their lists to help students who haven't come up with any ideas.

Plan

B (15 minutes)

1. Direct students to look through their list of risks and choose one they would like to write about.

2. Have students work individually to complete their outlines. Monitor and provide feedback.

▶ *Reading and Writing 3, page 152*

Write

C (15 minutes)

1. Direct students to look at the Self-Assessment checklist on p. 152. Go over each item on the checklist. Remind students that you will be using a similar rubric to evaluate their writing.

2. Ask students to work individually to write their essays.

Alternative Unit Assignments

Assign or have students choose one of these assignments to do instead of, or in addition to, the Unit Assignment.

1. Do you know someone who has taken a risk, either a personal, professional or financial one? Write about this person, the risk he or she took, and the outcome.

2. Think of an activity involving risk that you would like to try. Describe what the risk would be and why you would like to try the activity.

 For an additional Unit Assignment, have students visit *Q Online Practice*.

Revise and Edit

Peer Review

A (15 minutes)

1. Pair students and direct them to read each other's work

2. Ask students to answer the questions and discuss them.

3. Give students suggestions for how to give helpful feedback: *This is a good introduction, but I don't think the concluding statement explains why this risk was important to you.*

Rewrite

B (10 minutes)

Students should review their partners' answers from A and rewrite their paragraphs accordingly.

Edit

C (10 minutes)

1. Direct students to read and complete the Self-Assessment checklist. They should be prepared to hand in their work or discuss it in class.

2. Ask for a show of hands for how many students gave all or mostly *yes* answers.

3. Use the Unit Assignment Rubric on p. 75 in this *Teacher's Handbook* to score each student's assignment.

4. Alternatively, divide the class into large groups and have students read their paragraphs to their group. Pass out copies of the Unit Assignment Rubric and have students grade each other.

▶ *Reading and Writing 3, page 153*

Track Your Success (5 minutes)

1. Have students circle the words they have learned in this unit. Suggest that students go back through the unit to review any words they have forgotten.

2. Have students check the skills they have mastered. If students need more practice to feel confident about their proficiency in a skill, point out the page numbers and encourage them to review.

3. Read the Learning Outcome aloud. Ask students if they feel that they have met the outcome.

Unit Assignment Rubric

Student name: _____

Date: _____

Unit Assignment: *Write a narrative essay describing a risk you have taken.*

20 points = Essay element was completely successful (at least 90% of the time).
15 points = Essay element was mostly successful (at least 70% of the time).
10 points = Essay element was partially successful (at least 50% of the time).
 0 points = Essay element was not successful.

Narrative Essay	20 points	15 points	10 points	0 points
Student used punctuation, spelling, and word forms correctly in the narrative essay.				
Essay includes vocabulary from the unit.				
Essay begins with an introductory paragraph that gives the reason the person took the risk and any important background information.				
Essay has two body paragraphs that include events and details.				
Student used time frames (shifts in verbs) correctly.				

Total points: _____

Comments:

Unit QUESTION
How can we make cities better places to live?

Cities/Urban Lives

READING • making inferences
VOCABULARY • participles as adjectives
WRITING • writing a problem/solution essay; thesis statements
GRAMMAR • passive voice

LEARNING OUTCOME

Write a problem/solution essay describing how your city can become a better place to live.

▶ *Reading and Writing 3, pages 154–155*
Preview the Unit

Learning Outcome

1. Ask for a volunteer to read the unit skills, then the unit learning outcome.

2. Explain: *This is what you are expected to be able to do by the unit's end. The learning outcome explains how you are going to be evaluated. With this outcome in mind, you should focus on learning these skills (Reading, Vocabulary, Writing, Grammar) that will support your goal of writing a problem/solution essay describing how your city can become a better place to live. This can also help you act as mentors in the classroom to help the other students meet this outcome.*

A (15 minutes)

1. To get students thinking about the topic, elicit some problems that cities typically have. Write the problems on the board, sorting them into different categories, such as *Transportation, Housing, Public Areas,* and *Services.*

2. Put students in pairs or small groups to discuss the first two questions.

3. Call on volunteers to share their ideas with the class. Ask follow-up questions: *What is the best thing about living in this city? What is the worst thing?*

4. Focus students' attention on the photo. Have a volunteer describe the photo to the class. Read the question aloud.

Activity A Answers, p. 155
Answers will vary. Possible answers:
1. Yes, I like where I live because it's exciting, there's a lot to do, and I know all my neighbors./No, I don't like where I live because it's noisy, crowded, and dirty.
2. Yes, I agree because "green" cities are cleaner and have less pollution.
3. She is borrowing a city bike. It's better for the environment than a car.

B (20 minutes)

1. Label four pieces of poster paper with the problem categories from Activity A. You may want to replace one of those categories with "Other." Place the pieces of paper in the corners of the room.

2. Ask students to read and consider the Unit Question for a moment. Then have a quarter of the class stand in each corner.

3. Direct the students in each corner to talk amongst themselves and list one or two problems on the paper for that category. Encourage students to be specific if it helps them generate ideas, e.g., *line of cars waiting to turn left at 2nd St. in the a.m.* vs. *traffic.* After students have listed a couple of problems, have the groups switch corners. Repeat the process, rotating the groups until they have written at least one problem on every paper.

4. On the last rotation, ask the groups to discuss solutions to the problems on the paper and write them down. Then call on volunteers from each corner to read the problems from the paper and share the group's solutions with the class.

5. Leave the posters up for students to refer back to at the end of the unit.

Activity B Answers, p. 155

Answers will vary. Possible answers:

Lower-level: have more buses; make more parks

Mid-level: Mix residential and business areas so people don't have to drive; Put in public swimming pools so that everyone has access to a pool.

Higher-level: (Students may be able to provide more specific suggestions with reasons.) They should put in a subway below Howard St. because the buses move down it very slowly, and it's crowded all day.

The Q Classroom (5 minutes)

CD 2, Track 11

1. Play The Q Classroom. Use the example from the audio to help students continue the conversation. Ask: *How did the students answer the question? Do you agree or disagree with their ideas? Why?*

2. Ask students to look over the problems and solutions they wrote for Activity B. Give them time to add any ideas they liked from the audio.

▶ *Reading and Writing 3, page 156*

C (5 minutes)

1. Elicit the meaning of *footprint*. Read the introductory paragraph about carbon footprints. Ask students what kinds of activities would make someone's personal carbon footprint larger.

2. Have students work individually to complete the survey. Discuss the items on the survey and elicit the connections between the activities and the carbon footprint. For example, ask: *How does eating meat/using plastic or paper bags/living in a house lead to a bigger carbon footprint?*

D (10 minutes)

1. Ask students to discuss their survey results with a partner.

2. Elicit students' ideas about reducing their carbon footprint.

EXPANSION ACTIVITY: Discussing Your Carbon Footprint (5 minutes)

Talk about the carbon footprint of your class or school. Pair students or ask them to continue working with their partners from Activity D to talk about these topics with regards to the school: heating/cooling; recycling; transportation; electricity and water use; room efficiency. Have students share their ideas and any suggestions they have about how the school could reduce its carbon footprint.

▶ *Reading and Writing 3, page 157*

READING

READING 1: New Zero-Carbon City to Be Built

VOCABULARY (15 minutes)

1. Direct students to read the words and definitions in the box. Say each word and use it in a sample sentence or elicit one from a volunteer who is familiar with the word. For example, *His car broke down, so his only **alternative** was to ride the bus.* Ask students to complete the email with the words from the box.

2. Have pairs compare answers. Elicit answers from volunteers. Have students underline context clues in the email that helped them know which word belonged in each blank. Then have students repeat the vocabulary words. Highlight the syllable in each word that receives primary stress.

> **MULTILEVEL OPTION**
>
> Group lower-level students and assist them with the task. Read the email aloud and elicit the answers from the group, clearing up questions as you go.
>
> Have higher-level students complete the activity individually and then compare answers with a partner. Assign one or two words to each pair and ask them to write sentences with the words. Have volunteers write their sentences on the board. Correct the sentences with the whole class, focusing on the use of the word rather than other grammatical issues.

Vocabulary Answers, pp. 157–158

1. release;
2. waste;
3. recycling;
4. alternative;
5. environmentally;
6. chiefly;
7. renewable;
8. unique;
9. compete;
10. resources

 For additional practice with the vocabulary, have students visit *Q Online Practice*.

▶ *Reading and Writing 3, pages 159*

PREVIEW READING 1 (5 minutes)

1. Have students read the first and last paragraphs of the article and check their predictions.

2. Tell them they should review their predictions after reading.

> **Preview Reading 1 Answer, p. 159**
> Checked: solar

Reading 1 Background Note

Although they are not as ambitious as Masdar City, a number of cities around the world have dramatically reduced their carbon footprint. The city of Malmo, Sweden, has a district run entirely on renewable resources. This district is known for its roof gardens and emission-free electric street trains. Copenhagen, Denmark, has a water-pollution monitoring system to alert officials when pollution levels are too high, and it also has 5,600 windmills. Portland, Oregon, encourages pedestrian and bicycle traffic with its mix of green and urban areas, has a large number of sustainable public buildings, and relies mainly on renewable resources for its energy. Vancouver, Canada, is the world's leading user of hydroelectric energy, and Reykjavik, Iceland, is working toward becoming an all-hydrogen economy.

For students interested in learning more about their personal carbon footprint, there are a number of "carbon footprint calculators" online.

READ (20 minutes)

 CD 2, Track 12

1. Instruct students to read the article and refer to the glossed words. Tell them to mark any unknown vocabulary but to continue reading. Ask them to set their pens down or look up when they've completed the article.

2. When most students have finished reading, elicit and discuss their vocabulary questions.

3. Play the audio and ask students to read along silently.

▶ *Reading and Writing 3, page 161*

MAIN IDEAS (10 minutes)

1. Ask students to read the sentences and circle the completions.

2. Go over the answers with the class. Have students point out the information in the text that helped them choose the right answer.

> **Main Ideas Answers, p. 161**
> **1.** b; **2.** b; **3.** c; **4.** b

DETAILS (10 minutes)

1. Direct students to work individually to answer the questions.

2. Elicit the answers from volunteers.

> **Details Answers, pp. 161–162**
> **1.** $22 billion;
> **2.** 6 square kilometers;
> **3.** more than 50,000;
> **4.** because there will be a personal rapid transit system;
> **5.** 1,500;
> **6.** They make solar panels;
> **7.** annoyed55;
> **8.** realitysam

 For additional practice with reading comprehension, have students visit *Q Online Practice*.

▶ *Reading and Writing 3, page 162*

WHAT DO YOU THINK? (20 minutes)

1. Ask students to read the questions and reflect on their answers.

2. Seat students in small groups and assign roles: a group leader to make sure everyone contributes, a note-taker to record the group's ideas, a reporter to share the group's ideas with the class, and a timekeeper to watch the clock.

3. Give students five minutes to discuss the questions. Call time if conversations are winding down. Allow them an extra minute or two if necessary.

4. Call on each group's reporter to share ideas with the class.

5. Have each student choose one of the questions and write five to eight sentences in response.

6. Call on volunteers to share their responses with the class.

What Do You Think? Answers, p. 162

Answers will vary. Possible answers:

1. Yes I would. The air would be clean, and it would be a good place to walk. It would be safer to ride my bike if there were no cars. There would be less traffic noise. And we could use space for parks instead of parking lots and garages.

2. Advantages: The city would be new, clean, and pleasant to walk in. Transportation would be convenient, and you'd never have to look for parking. Disadvantages: Everything would be new. The city has nothing of historical interest. Neighbors wouldn't have known each other long.

3. I agree with abouttimesue28. I think it's very exciting that they're doing this project. Masdar has the money to try something like this. I think that when other cities see what Masdar did, they'll try these things, too. It will be good for the earth if many cities start using solar power and PRTs.

Learning Outcome

Use the learning outcome to frame the purpose and relevance of Reading 1. Ask: *What did you learn from Reading 1 that will help you write about improving your city?* (Students learned some ideas for reducing the carbon footprint of a city. They may want to use these ideas in their problem/solution essay.)

Reading Skill: Making inferences
(5 minutes)

1. Direct students to read the information about inferences.

2. Ask: *What do you do when you make an inference?* Discuss the expression *Read between the lines.*

3. Write two sentences on the board, e.g., *Mary put the cup of coffee down in front of the customer. "Thanks Mary," he said with a smile.* Ask students what they can infer from the sentences. (Mary is a waitress. The customer either knows her, or she's wearing a nametag. The customer likes her.) Point out that this information is "between the lines" because it isn't actually stated.

▶ *Reading and Writing 3, page 163*

A (5 minutes)

1. Direct students to read the statements. Ask them to work individually to circle the correct inference.

2. Call on volunteers for the answers. Ask them to explain their answers, e.g., "More people means more trains and buses."

Reading Skill A Answers, p. 163
1. a; **2.** b; **3.** a; **4.** b

B (10 minutes)

1. Read the directions and have students complete the activity individually. Ask them to compare their answers with a partner.

2. Go over the answers with the class.

Reading Skill B Answers, p. 163
(checked):
3. The city is situated so that it gets a great deal of sun on one side;
4. The entire city will be powered by these renewable forms of energy.

 For additional practice with making inferences, have students visit *Q Online Practice.*

▶ *Reading and Writing 3, page 164*

READING 2: "Out of the Box" Ideas for Greener Cities

VOCABULARY (15 minutes)

1. Direct students to read the sentences and guess from context what they think the word in bold means. Then have them circle the word or phrase that best matches the bold word.

2. Have students compare their answers with a partner.

3. Elicit the answers from volunteers. Have students repeat the pronunciation of the bold words. Highlight the syllable that receives primary stress in each word.

Vocabulary Answers, p. 164
1. effective; **2.** create; **3.** fruits and vegetables;
4. city; **5.** usual; **6.** risk; **7.** dirty; **8.** fix;
9. well-being; **10.** new

 For additional practice with the vocabulary, have students visit *Q Online Practice.*

▶ *Reading and Writing 3, page 165*

PREVIEW READING 2 (5 minutes)

1. Have students read the first sentence of each paragraph and check their predictions.

2. Tell students they should review their predictions after reading.

> **Preview Reading Answer, p. 165**
> (checked): transportation, planting/parks/trees, pollution

Reading 2 Background Note

Although indoor farming hasn't taken off yet, more and more cities are embracing urban agriculture for a variety of reasons. First of all, food grown in a city doesn't have to be transported as far, which reduces carbon emissions. Secondly, urban farming creates "green space" in cities and teaches children about agriculture. Finally, neighborhoods develop a sense of community when neighbors work together in community gardens. Encourage students to research urban agriculture in the cities where they live.

READ (5 minutes)

 CD 2, Track 13

1. Instruct students to read the article and refer to the glossed words. Tell them to mark any unknown vocabulary but to continue reading. Ask them to set their pens down or look up when they've completed the article.

2. When most students have finished reading, elicit and discuss their vocabulary questions.

3. Play the audio and ask students to read along silently.

▶ *Reading and Writing 3, page 167*

MAIN IDEAS (15 minutes)

1. Ask students to read the sentences and label them *MI* or *SD*. Have them compare their answers with a partner.

2. Go over the answers with the class.

> **Main Idea Answers, p. 167**
> **2.** MI; **3.** SD; **4.** MI; **5.** SD;
> **6.** SD; **7.** MI; **8.** SD

DETAILS (10 minutes)

1. Direct students to write the advantages in the correct column of the chart.

2. Call on volunteers for the answers. Discuss how some advantages could go in multiple columns.

> **Details Answers, p. 167**
> Urban Farming: floods and droughts won't affect crops, no herbicides or pesticides, more "green space"
> Tearing Down Highways: quality of life improved, a decrease in CO_2 emissions, more "green space"
> "Bicing" Program: fewer cars in the city, a decrease in CO_2 emissions

 For additional practice with reading comprehension, have students visit *Q Online Practice.*

▶ *Reading and Writing 3, page 168*

Q WHAT DO YOU THINK?

A (15 minutes)

1. Ask students to read the questions and reflect on their answers.

2. Seat students in small groups and assign roles: a group leader to make sure everyone contributes, a note-taker to record the group's ideas, a reporter to share the group's ideas with the class, and a timekeeper to watch the clock.

3. Give students five minutes to discuss the questions. Call time if conversations are winding down. Allow them an extra minute or two if necessary.

4. Call on each group's reporter to share their responses with the class.

> **Activity A Answers, p. 168**
> Possible answers:
> **1.** Urban farming, because I'd like to eat locally-grown food, but it's hard to do in a big city. The "bicing" program because I love to ride a bike, but it's not convenient to take my bike on public transportation.
> **2.** I think we should tear down a highway and put in more public transportation because this city needs more green space.

Critical Thinking Tip (5 minutes)

1. Have a student read the tip aloud. Explain: *We have to make choices every day. We use our own experience and knowledge to consider why one option might be better than other options.*

2. Ask: *In your everyday life, when do you need to choose one thing over other things?*

Evaluate Information

Take students through the process of choosing an answer to the question in Activity B. Write each method for lowering carbon emissions on the board, and elicit ways that each one will improve people's quality of life. For example, under "eliminating the dependence on cars," some improvements could be: *People will be healthier because they will walk or bicycle more; People will socialize more if they aren't alone in their cars; Communities will become closer because people won't travel as far for everyday shopping needs; The streets and the air will be cleaner; Not as much space will be taken up by ugly roads; People won't spend so much money on cars,* etc. After students have brainstormed a list for each topic, have them compare both the length of the list and the importance of the results. Point out that a good evaluation requires careful consideration of the details. Ask if anyone would change their original answer based on the results of the discussion.

B (5 minutes)

1. Tell the students that they should think about both Reading 1 and Reading 2 as they answer the question in Activity B. Students will write five to eight sentences in response to the question.

2. Ask students to read their sentences with a partner.

3. Call on each pair to share their responses with the class.

   Activity B Answer, p. 168
   Possible answer:
   I think eliminating the dependence on cars will improve people's quality of life the most. It will reduce pollution and noise. It will cut down on use of fossil fuels. It will also make more "green space" possible since fewer roads will be needed. Also, people will be healthier because they will walk or bicycle instead.

Learning Outcome

Use the learning outcome to frame the purpose and relevance of Readings 1 and 2. Ask: *What did you learn from Readings 1 and 2 that prepares you to write about a way to improve your city?* (Students read about many ways to make a city more environmentally friendly. They may incorporate some of these ideas into their problem/solution essay.)

Vocabulary Skill: Participles as adjectives (15 minutes)

1. Have students read the information about participles as adjectives.

2. Check comprehension by eliciting participle forms of several verbs, e.g., *frighten, break, satisfy.* Ask students to use the participle forms as adjectives (e.g. *the frightened child, the broken bell, the satisfied customer*).

A (5 minutes)

1. Direct students to read the sentences and write *adjective* or *verb* for each underlined word.

2. Call on volunteers for the answers.

   Vocabulary Skill Answers, p. 168–169
   2. verb;   **3.** adjective;   **4.** verb;
   5. adjective;   **6.** verb;   **7.** verb;
   8. adjective;   **9.** verb;   **10.** adjective

Skill Note

- Not all past participles can be used as adjectives before nouns, e.g., you can say *lost child* but not *found child.*

- Most (but not all) past participles have a passive meaning when they are used as adjectives, e.g., a *broken* window, the *invited* guests, the *bored* student.

- Students will probably be familiar with past-participle adjectives describing how people feel, e.g., *amused, astonished, confused, delighted, depressed, distressed, embarrassed, excited, frightened, interested, satisfied, shocked, surprised, tired, worried.* These are often confused with their present-participle (*-ing* form) counterparts, which describe people or things that cause feelings.

▶ *Reading and Writing 3, page 169*

B (15 minutes)

1. Direct students to work with a partner to write sentences using five words from Activity A. Tell them that at least three of the words should be used as adjectives.

2. Ask every pair to choose one sentence to write on the board. Correct the sentences as a class.

Activity B Answers, p. 169

Answers will vary. Possible answers:
1. The scientists conducted a controlled experiment.
2. The increased number of students means we need more classes.
3. The reduced prices brought in a lot of customers.
4. The polluted air made me feel sick.
5. I gave my worn jeans to my sister.

 For additional practice with participles as adjectives, have students visit *Q Online Practice*.

▶ *Reading and Writing 3, page 170*

WRITING

21ST CENTURY SKILLS

Employers put a high value on employees with problem-solving skills. Finding people who can report problems is easy, but finding those who can identify and propose solutions is another matter. Point out to students that there are many situations in which it's important to be able to clearly state problems and to identify multiple solutions. Ask them to identify a problem in your community or at your school and write it on the board. Elicit solutions and point out that it may be easy to come up with one solution, but that multiple solutions are more useful because the "obvious" solution may not be possible. Ask students how they can go about finding solutions to a problem (e.g., brainstorming with others, asking someone with experience, doing research).

Writing Skill: Writing a problem/solution essay; thesis statements (10 minutes)

1. Direct students to read the first paragraph about problem/solution essays. Check comprehension: *What is a problem/solution essay? What does a thesis statement do? What is described in the body paragraphs? What does the concluding paragraph do?*

2. Have students read the paragraph about thesis statements and the example. Ask: *What problem is this essay about? What is the main idea of the essay?*

3. Direct students to read the information about the body of the essay and the example topic sentences. Elicit the solution that each paragraph will discuss. Ask students to guess what details might follow each thesis statements.

1. Read the tip aloud.

2. Ask students to find the introductory phrases used in the sample topic sentences (*One way, Another way, Finally*). Tell them to keep these phrases in mind when it's time to write their essays.

▶ *Reading and Writing 3, page 171*

A (5 minutes)

1. Direct students to read the problem/solution essay.

2. Check comprehension. *What problem is the writer talking about? How many solutions does the writer give?*

B (5 minutes)

1. Direct students to work with a partner to read the questions and do the activity

2. Monitor and provide feedback while the pairs are working.

3. Discuss the solutions suggested by the writer and ask students to share their opinions about them. Elicit any other solutions students have to the problem of downtown traffic.

Activity B Answers, pp. 171–172

1. (underlined): Currently, our downtown area is not a pleasant place to be because of the congestion, and this is a serious situation that needs to be addressed immediately.
2. (bracketed): ban passenger cars from the downtown area.
3. (bracketed): provide alternative forms of transportation.
4. (bracketed): encourage people to ride bikes.

5. Yes. (underlined): Our downtown area has become extremely crowded in recent years. (circled): Eliminating cars from downtown, introducing a streetcar system, and creating bike lanes....
6. Answers will vary. Possible answers: Yes, I agree because a crowded downtown would be much nicer without cars./No, I don't agree because I don't think it's realistic for people to give up their cars.

 For additional practice with writing a problem/solution essay, have students visit *Q Online Practice*.

▶ *Reading and Writing 3, page 172*

Grammar: Passive voice (10 minutes)

1. Read the information about passive sentences aloud and go over the examples.

2. Check comprehension by writing passive sentences on the board. *The river was buried under a highway. The highway was used by thousands of people. Eventually, the highway was destroyed and the river was restored.* Elicit active versions of the sentences. Discuss the reasons for the passive choice. (The person or agency that did the action is not important. The focus is on what happened to the river and the highway.)

Skill Note

The passive voice is sometimes confusing to students because it can be formed in any tense and because the verb *be* and the past participle are used in other structures. Help students understand how the tenses are used by writing active and passive sentences on the board:

Past: The state built a nuclear power plant.

          A nuclear power plant <u>was</u> built (by the state.)

Present: Cars cause a lot of pollution.

          A lot of pollution <u>is</u> caused by cars.

Future: The city will tear down old buildings.

          Old buildings <u>will be</u> torn down.

Point out that the tense is shown in the verb *be* and that this applies to passive voice in any tense (*can be, has been, is being,* etc.)

▶ *Reading and Writing 3, page 173*

A (10 minutes)

1. Ask students to work with a partner to look through the reading and find three examples of passive sentences.

2. Elicit the answers from volunteers. Students may have questions about "Our downtown area is congested," and "The air is filled with exhaust fumes." In both of these cases, the *–ed* form is considered to be a stative adjective because the focus is on the condition of being congested/filled.

> **Activity A Answers, p. 173**
> **1.** ...this is a serious situation that needs to be addressed immediately;
> **2.** The width of the sidewalks could be expanded...;
> **3.** With fewer emissions, C0₂ emissions would be lowered...; Bike racks could be built...

Tip for Success (5 minutes)

1. Read the tip aloud.

2. If possible, bring in example passive sentences from current news stories to share with students. Write them on the board and elicit active versions. Discuss why the writer chose the passive voice.

B (10 minutes)

1. Ask students to work individually to write the sentences. Then have them compare their sentences with a partner.

2. Call on volunteers to read their sentences aloud.

> **Activity B Answers, p. 173**
> **2.** A vegetable farm was planted in a 20-story skyscraper.
> **3.** The energy for the construction of the city was produced by solar panels.
> **4.** The entire highway was torn down in 12 months.
> **5.** A beautiful park was built in the area that was once an eyesore.

MULTILEVEL OPTION

Have lower-level students work in pairs to complete the activity, and assist these pairs as necessary. When higher-level students finish, ask them to write an original passive-voice sentence.

 For additional practice with passive voice, have students visit *Q Online Practice*.

▶ *Reading and Writing 3, page 174*

Q Unit Assignment:
Write a problem/solution essay

Unit Question (5 minutes)

Refer students back to the ideas they discussed at the beginning of the unit about making cities better places to live. Tell them they can use the ideas to help them write their Unit Assignment essays. Cue students if necessary by asking specific questions about the content of the unit: *How will Masdar City be a better city? What are some other cities doing to improve the quality of life for residents?*

Learning Outcome

1. Tie the Unit Assignment to the unit learning outcome. Say: *The outcome for this unit is to write a problem/solution essay about how your city can become a better place to live. This Unit Assignment is going to let you show your skill in using the vocabulary from the unit, adjectives, the passive voice, and correct essay format.*

2. Explain that you are going to use a rubric similar to their Self-Assessment checklist on p. 176 to grade their Unit Assignment. You can also share a copy of the Unit Assignment Rubric (on p. 86 of this *Teacher's Handbook*) with the students.

Plan and Write

Brainstorm

A (15 minutes)

Ask students to look back at the posters they created at the beginning of the unit to answer the Unit Question. Elicit problems in the city, school, or neighborhood that you have discussed throughout the unit. Ask students to choose one problem and write down as many solutions as they can think of.

Plan

B (15 minutes)

1. Direct students to read through what they have written and circle their three best solutions.

2. Have students work individually to complete their outlines. Monitor and provide feedback.

▶ *Reading and Writing 3, page 175*

Write

C (15 minutes)

1. Direct students to look at the Self-Assessment checklist on p. 176. Go over the items on the checklist. Remind them that you will be using a similar rubric to evaluate their writing.

2. Ask students to work individually to write their essays.

Alternative Unit Assignments

Assign or have students choose one of these assignments to do instead of, or in addition to, the Unit Assignment.

1. Write about a problem in your school or town or somewhere else in the world that was solved. Describe the problem and how it was solved.

2. Research cities that have solved an environmental problem in an unusual way. Write a paragraph describing the problem and the solution.

 For an additional Unit Assignment, have students visit *Q Online Practice*.

▶ *Reading and Writing 3, page 176*

Revise and Edit

Peer Review

A (15 minutes)

1. Pair students and direct them to read each other's work.

2. Ask students to answer the questions and discuss them.

3. Give students suggestions for how to give helpful feedback: *The problems and solutions in the body are good, but you didn't summarize them in the conclusion.*

Rewrite

B (10 minutes)

Students should review their partners' answers from A and rewrite their paragraphs accordingly.

Edit

C (10 minutes)

1. Direct students to read and complete the Self-Assessment checklist. They should be prepared to hand in their work or discuss it in class.

2. Ask for a show of hands for how many students gave all or mostly *yes* answers.

3. Use the Unit Assignment Rubric on p. 86 in this *Teacher's Handbook* to score each student's assignment.

4. Alternatively, divide the class into large groups and have students read their paragraphs to their group. Pass out copies of the Unit Assignment Rubric and have students grade each other.

▶ *Reading and Writing 3, page 177*

Track Your Success (5 minutes)

1. Have students circle the words they have learned in this unit. Suggest that students go back through the unit to review any words they have forgotten.

2. Have students check the skills they have mastered. If students need more practice to feel confident about their proficiency in a skill, point out the page numbers and encourage them to review.

3. Read the Learning Outcome aloud. Ask students if they feel that they have met the outcome.

Unit Assignment Rubric

Student name: _____

Date: _____

Unit Assignment: *Write a problem/solution essay describing how your city can become a better place to live.*

20 points = Essay element was completely successful (at least 90% of the time).
15 points = Essay element was mostly successful (at least 70% of the time).
10 points = Essay element was partially successful (at least 50% of the time).
 0 points = Essay element was not successful.

Problem/Solution Essay	20 points	15 points	10 points	0 points
Student clearly described how his/her city can become a better place to live.				
Essay includes vocabulary from the unit.				
Essay includes a thesis statement that states a problem and a concluding paragraph that summarizes the problem and solutions.				
Essay includes at least two body paragraphs with solutions.				
Student used passive voice and participles as adjectives correctly.				

Total points: _____

Comments:

Unit QUESTION

How can a small amount of money make a big difference?

Money

READING • using a timeline
VOCABULARY • collocations with nouns
WRITING • writing a cause/effect essay
GRAMMAR • complex sentences to show cause and effect

LEARNING OUTCOME

Write a cause/effect essay explaining how a small amount of money can make a big difference.

▶ *Reading and Writing 3, pages 178–179*

Preview the Unit

Learning Outcome

1. Ask for a volunteer to read the unit skills, then the unit learning outcome.

2. Explain: *This is what you are expected to be able to do by the unit's end. The learning outcome explains how you are going to be evaluated. With this outcome in mind, you should focus on learning these skills (Reading, Vocabulary, Writing, Grammar) that will support your goal of writing a cause/effect essay explaining how a small amount of money can make a big difference. This can also help you act as mentors in the classroom to help the other students meet this outcome.*

A (15 minutes)

1. To get students thinking about the topic, elicit the names of any organizations they know of that help people. If necessary, ask questions to get them started, e.g., *Who gives food to people who need it in this city? Where can you buy used clothing? Do you know of an organization that provides medical help to people?*

2. Put students in pairs or small groups to discuss the first two questions.

3. Call on volunteers to share their ideas with the class. Ask follow-up questions, e.g., *What kinds of help do people in this area need? What about people in other countries? How do you decide who to give to?*

4. Focus students' attention on the photo. Have a volunteer describe the photo to the class. Read the question aloud.

Activity A Answers, p. 179

Answers will vary. Possible answers:

1. Yes, I've given money during an emergency / to strangers on the street / in response to a mailed request / to a local organization that helps women and children / by buying a product at the store. It made me feel good / useful.

2. Large charities; religious institutions; schools; youth activities/teams; clinics and medical organizations; arts and cultural organizations; political organizations, environmental groups. How donated money is used: provide food, clothing, or sports/ medical equipment to people who need it; host art exhibits and cultural events; pay for campaign expenses; help animals near extinction, etc.

3. Mosquito nets are being given away.

B (20 minutes)

1. Introduce the Unit Question, *How can a small amount of money make a big difference?* Ask related information questions or questions about personal experience to help students prepare for answering the more abstract unit question. *How much money do you think most people give to [one of the organizations students mentioned]? Do you think that amount of money helps? How?*

2. Put students in small groups and give each group a piece of poster paper and a marker.

3. Give students a minute to silently consider their answers to the Unit Question. Tell students to pass the paper and marker around the group. Each group member should write a different answer to the question. Encourage them to help one another.

4. Ask each group to share their answers with the class. Point out similarities and differences among the answers. If answers from different groups are similar, make a class list that incorporates all of the answers. Post the list to refer to later in the unit.

Activity B Answers, p. 179

Answers will vary. Possible answers:
Lower-level answers: If many people give, it helps a lot.
Mid-level answers: Some improvements are not very expensive. If money is spent well, it goes a long way.
Higher-level answers: (Students may be able to describe examples.) When people donate books and hours to a reading program for children, the children benefit greatly for not much money.

The Q Classroom (5 minutes)

🔊 CD 3, Track 2

1. Play The Q Classroom. Use the example from the audio to help students continue the conversation. Ask: *How did the students answer the question? Do you agree or disagree with their ideas? Why?*

2. Ask students to look over the ideas they wrote for Activity B. Give them time to add new ideas to their notes.

▶ *Reading and Writing 3, page 180*

C (5 minutes)

1. Ask students to look at the pictures and match them to the results in the box.

2. Elicit the answers. Find out if students have any idea how much each animal produces. (A goat averages about 3 quarts of milk a day for 10 months; An average honeybee hive produces about 30 lbs. of honey a season; One sheep produces between 100 and 300 lbs. of wool a year; Over the course of its lifetime (about 2.5 years), one hen may lay up to 900 eggs. It takes 2,000 to 3,000 silkworm cocoons to make a pound of silk.)

Activity C Answers, p. 180
A. milk;   **B.** honey;   **C.** wool;   **D.** eggs;
E. silk;   **F.** education

D (10 minutes)

1. Read the saying aloud. Find out if students have a comparable saying in their native language.

2. Direct them to work with a partner to discuss the question. Call on volunteers for their ideas.

▶ *Reading and Writing 3, page 181*

READING

READING 1: How a Ugandan Girl Got an Education

VOCABULARY (15 minutes)

1. Have partners read the sentences and use context clues to try to guess what each word in bold means or think of a synonym for the word. Then have them match the bold words to the definitions.

2. Call on volunteers to read the sentences aloud. Answer any questions about definitions and provide or elicit additional examples of the words in context. Pronounce and have students repeat the words. Highlight the stressed syllable in each word.

3. Have the pairs read the sentences together.

> **MULTILEVEL OPTION**
>
> Group lower-level students and assist them with the task. Point out context clues and ask questions to help students connect to the vocabulary, e.g., *Finishing school and starting a job is a change, or* **transition.** *What other* **transitions** *do people make in life?*
>
> Have higher-level students complete the activity individually and then compare answers with a partner. Assign two words to each pair and ask them to write an example sentence for each word. Have volunteers write one of their sentences on the board.

Vocabulary Answers, pp. 181–182
a. adjustment;   **b.** attend;   **c.** commitment;
d. distribute;   **e.** extremely;   **f.** generosity;
g. inspire;   **h.** owe;   **i.** proud;
j. transition

 For additional practice with the vocabulary, have students visit *Q Online Practice.*

▶ *Reading and Writing 3, page 182*

PREVIEW READING 1 (5 minutes)

1. Ask students to read the introductory information. Show students the location of Uganda on a world map or globe.

2. Direct students to read the first and last paragraphs and to check their predictions. Tell them to look back at their predictions after they have read the article.

> **Preview Reading 1 Answer, p. 182**
> (checked): an animal

Reading 1 Background Note

The Internet has made it easy for people to donate small amounts of money toward a specific cause or person rather than to a large charity that disperses the money to unknown recipients. One popular method of helping people in need is through "microloans" or "microfinance," where a person invests a small amount of money to help a would-be entrepreneur. Potential investors can look through the profiles of people who are hoping to start or build a business but too poor to receive traditional financing and choose whom to lend a small amount of money to. The person receiving the money is expected to pay it back according to a schedule set up by the lending institution. When investors get their money back, they can withdraw it or lend it to another entrepreneur.

▶ *Reading and Writing 3, page 183*

READ (20 minutes)

🔊 CD 3, Track 3

1. Instruct students to read the article. Remind them to refer to the glossed words. Tell them to mark any unknown vocabulary but to continue reading. Ask them to set their pens down or look up when they've completed the article.

2. When most students have finished reading, elicit and discuss their vocabulary questions.

3. Play the audio and ask students to read along silently.

▶ *Reading and Writing 3, page 184*

MAIN IDEAS (10 minutes)

1. Ask students to read the statements and work individually to complete the activity. Tell them to underline the information in each paragraph where they find the main idea.

2. Call on volunteers for the answers. Point out that the main idea can be found at the beginning of each paragraph.

> **Main Ideas Answers, p. 184**
> **1.** 2; **2.** 4; **3.** 7; **4.** 3; **5.** 5

▶ *Reading and Writing 3, page 185*

DETAILS (10 minutes)

1. Direct students to read the statements and label them *T* or *F*. Encourage them to circle the information in the article that helped them choose each answer.

2. Call on volunteers for the answers. Elicit corrections for the false statements.

> **Details Answers, p. 185**
> **1.** F Beatrice couldn't see the value in the goat.
> **2.** T;
> **3.** T;
> **4.** F Beatrice was an excellent student even though she was so much older than the other students.
> **5.** F ...called *Beatrice's Goat*;
> **6.** F The biggest adjustment...was the weather.
> **7.** T;
> **8.** T

 For additional practice with reading comprehension, have students visit *Q Online Practice*.

Q WHAT DO YOU THINK? (20 minutes)

1. Ask students to read the questions and reflect on their answers.

2. Seat the students in small groups and assign roles: a group leader to make sure everyone contributes, a note-taker to record the group's ideas, a reporter to share the group's ideas with the class, and a timekeeper to watch the clock.

3. Give students five minutes to discuss the questions. Call time if conversations are winding down. Allow them an extra minute or two if necessary.

4. Call on each group's reporter to share ideas with the class.

5. Have each student choose one of the questions and write five to eight sentences in response.

6. Call on volunteers to share their responses with the class.

MULTILEVEL OPTION

Seat students in mixed-ability groups so that lower-level students can benefit from listening to higher-level students.

Allow lower-level students to write three sentences in response to the question they choose.

Ask higher-level students to write responses to more than one question.

What Do You Think? Answers, p. 185

Answers will vary. Possible answers:

1. The money paid for school. The story of Beatrice and her goat inspired the writers. The popularity of the book led to a book tour. The book tour led to meeting a woman who helped Beatrice get a scholarship to a preparatory school. The preparatory school studies led to a scholarship to college.

2. Beatrice has determination. Even though it seemed impossible for her to go to school, she never gave up. She is also intelligent. She was able to get good grades in school and do well in college. She must also have a good attitude. Even though it was hard for her to get used to living in a new county, she didn't complain, and she made the transition successfully.

3. I know someone who got a small loan from a friend and was able to start a catering business. First, she started with just a few customers. She did all the cooking and serving herself. When she started making money, she hired a couple of employees. They got more customers and catered bigger parties. Now she has 14 employees, and her business is very successful.

Learning Outcome

Use the learning outcome to frame the purpose and relevance of Reading 1. Ask: *What did you learn from Reading 1 that will help you write a cause/effect essay explaining how a small amount of money can make a big difference?* (Students learned that a simple gift of a goat led to a girl getting a good education and gaining skills to help her village. They also saw multiple causes and effects presented in a cause/effect essay.)

▶ *Reading and Writing 3, page 186*

Reading Skill: Using a timeline (5 minutes)

1. Direct students to read the information about timelines and study the example.

2. Check comprehension by asking questions: *What is a timeline? How can it help you with reading?*

Tip for Success (1 minute)

1. Read the tip aloud.

2. Ask students what kinds of texts they might want to use a timeline with (history texts, narratives).

A (15 minutes)

1. Have students read the title of the article. Find out if any of them have heard of Paul Newman. Show a picture of Paul Newman from the Internet or a picture of *Newman's Own* products.

2. Direct students to work individually to read the text and complete the timeline. Re-create the timeline on the board and have volunteers put in the events. Ask students which event was out of sequence in the text.

Reading Skill A Answers, pp. 186–187

1980-Newman and Hotchner bottled salad dressing for gifts.
1982-Profits are close to $400,000.
1988-The Hole in the Wall Gang camp is founded.
2008-More than 40 Newman's Own products are sold.

 For additional practice with timelines, have students visit *Q Online Practice*.

▶ *Reading and Writing 3, pages 187*

READING 2: Money Makes You Happy—If You Spend It on Others

VOCABULARY (15 minutes)

1. Direct students to read the sentences. Tell them to use the context clues from each sentence to circle the answer that best matches the meaning of the bold word.

2. Put students in pairs to compare answers. Elicit the answers from volunteers. Have students repeat the bold vocabulary words. Highlight the syllable in each word that receives primary stress. Discuss the context clues that helped students find the answers.

3. Ask questions to help students connect with the vocabulary: *Has the number of students here increased or **decreased** since school began? What other **remarkable** achievements have we talked about in this class?*

> **Vocabulary Answers, pp. 187–188**
> **1.** c; **2.** b; **3.** a; **4.** a; **5.** a;
> **6.** c; **7.** b; **8.** a; **9.** b

 For additional practice with the vocabulary, have students visit *Q Online Practice.*

▶ *Reading and Writing 3, page 189*

PREVIEW READING 2 (5 minutes)

1. Have students read the first sentence of each paragraph. Tell them to check their predictions.

2. Tell students they should review their answer after reading.

> **Preview Reading 2 Answer, p. 189**
> (checked): Giving away a small amount of money makes you happier than spending it on yourself.

Reading 2 Background Note

Students can make a connection between this article and the one on the biology of altruism on pp. 100–101. In the study discussed in the altruism article, it was shown that the pleasure centers in the brain light up when people make charitable contributions. The self-reported happiness in the studies discussed in this article is consistent with this brain research.

READ (20 minutes)

CD 3, Track 4

1. Instruct students to read the article and refer to the glossed words. Tell them to mark any unknown vocabulary but to continue reading. Ask them to set their pens down or look up when they've completed the article.

2. When most students have finished reading, elicit and discuss their vocabulary questions.

3. Play the audio and ask students to read along silently.

▶ *Reading and Writing 3, page 191*

MAIN IDEAS (10 minutes)

1. Ask students to read and complete the activity individually.

2. Elicit the answers from the class.

> **Main Ideas Answers, p. 191**
> **1.** a; **2.** b; **3.** a; **4.** a; **5.** a

▶ *Reading and Writing 3, page 192*

DETAILS (10 minutes)

1. Direct students to read the statements and complete the activity individually. Encourage students to underline the information in the text that validates their answers.

2. Go over the answers with the class.

> **Details Answers, p. 192**
> **1.** c; **2.** f; **3.** d; **4.** b; **5.** e; **6.** a

 For additional practice with reading comprehension, have students visit *Q Online Practice.*

WHAT DO YOU THINK?

A (15 minutes)

1. Ask students to read the questions and reflect on their answers.

2. Seat the students in small groups and assign roles: a group leader to make sure everyone contributes, a note-taker to record the group's ideas, a reporter to share the group's ideas with the class, and a timekeeper to watch the clock.

3. Give students five minutes to discuss the questions. Call time if conversations are winding down. Allow them an extra minute or two if necessary.

4. Call on each group's reporter to share ideas with the class.

5. Have each student choose one of the questions and write five to eight sentences in response.

6. Call on volunteers to share their responses with the class.

Activity A Answers, p. 192

Answers will vary. Possible answers:

1. Last month, there was a big fire in my city, and dozens of houses were burned down. The people who lived in those houses had nothing left. So I gave some money and some old clothes to a charity organization to help those people. I also went down there a few times to serve meals. It made me feel very happy to help those people.

2. When I was about fifteen years old, I really wanted a certain pair of jeans with pink hearts on the pockets. All the other girls at my school had those jeans, but my parents didn't want to buy them for me because they were expensive. So I saved all my babysitting money for three months to buy the jeans. Finally, I bought them. I was so excited to wear them, but when I wore them to school, no one even noticed. And by that time, all the girls were wearing a different brand of jeans!

B (5 minutes)

1. Tell the students that they should think about both Reading 1 and Reading 2 as they answer the questions in Activity B.

2. Ask students to discuss their answers in their groups.

3. Call on each group to share their responses with the class.

Activity B Answers, p. 192

Answers will vary. Possible answers:
They benefit equally. The giver benefits because they have long-lasting good feelings about themselves. The receiver benefits because they are able to make important changes in their lives.

Learning Outcome

Use the learning outcome to frame the purpose and relevance of Readings 1 and 2. Ask: *What did you learn from Readings 1 and 2 that will help you write about the effects of a small act of kindness?* (Students learned about how both the receiver and the giver of small gifts benefit. Students may want to incorporate these ideas into their cause/effect essays.)

▶ *Reading and Writing 3, page 193*

Vocabulary Skill:
Collocations with nouns (5 minutes)

1. Direct students to read the information about collocations.

2. Check comprehension: *What is a collocation? How does using collocations improve your writing?* Write sentence frames on the board using the sample collocations and elicit completions, e.g., *It was an act of kindness when ____. ____ always treated me with kindness. ____ benefited from the kindness of strangers.*

Skill Note

Collocations are particularly helpful to students when they are learning relatively low-frequency abstract nouns like *generosity* and *kindness*. The adjective forms of these words are more common in speaking, which makes the use of the noun in writing more challenging for students. Keep an eye out for these kinds of nouns and teach students several collocations to go with them. Examples from the vocabulary in this unit include *transition* (collocations: *abrupt, sudden, gradual, smooth; make a transition; a period of transition, a state of transition*) and *commitment* (*absolute, serious, personal; give/make/demonstrate a commitment; a lack of commitment*).

A (15 minutes)

1. Direct students to work individually to read the paragraph and underline the collocations from the skill box.

2. Go over the answers with the class.

Activity A Answers, p. 193

(underlined): treated with kindness; Through the generosity of; the kindness of strangers; act of generosity

B (15 minutes)

1. Have students work with a partner to write sentences using three of the collocations.

2. Ask volunteers to write one of their sentences on the board.

Activity B Answers, p. 193

Answers will vary. Possible answer:
When I came to the United States, many people treated me with kindness. People do small acts of kindness every day. Through the generosity of Heifer, Beatrice's family received a goat.

Allow lower-level students to use the sentence frames from the Vocabulary Skill presentation above for this activity. Additional frames: *Through the generosity of ____, I was able to ____. ____ showed extraordinary generosity when he / she ____. ____ has always shown generosity toward ____.*

 For additional practice with collocations with nouns, have students visit *Q Online Practice*.

▶ *Reading and Writing 3, page 194*

WRITING

21ST CENTURY SKILLS

Employers are looking for workers with critical thinking skills to identify causes and effects, and communication skills to explain them to others. Help students make the connection between their cause/effect essay and other situations where they might need to identify and explain causes and effects. For example, they may need to explain a way to increase sales to a manager, the benefits of a product to a customer, or the effects of a change in policy to a city official.

Writing Skill: Writing a cause/effect essay (20 minutes)

1. Direct students to read the information about cause/effect essays.

2. Check comprehension: *What are the parts of a cause/effect essay? What is the purpose of the introduction? What information is in the thesis statement? What information is in the body paragraphs? In the concluding paragraphs?*

3. Ask students to think back on the story about Beatrice and her goat. Tell them that the chain of events in the story was *caused* by Beatrice's mother asking for help. Elicit the results.

A (5 minutes)

1. Direct students to read the cause/effect essay and underline the thesis statement. Elicit any questions they have about vocabulary.

2. Ask a volunteer to read the thesis statement aloud.

Activity A Answer, pp. 194–195
(underlined): <u>A project like this one can result in new friendships, less loneliness, and the possible discovery of a career path!</u>

▶ *Reading and Writing 3, page 195*

Tip for Success (3 minutes)

1. Read the tip aloud.

2. Elicit possible topics for cause/effect essays in the various disciplines, e.g., in history: the cause and effects of an important battle; in science: the results of an experiment; the cause of a disease; in English: the results of an event on a character's life.

B (10 minutes)

1. Have students work individually to complete the graphic organizer.

2. Re-create the organizer on the board and ask volunteers to fill in the information.

Activity B Answers, p. 195
Cause: do an act of kindness for the elderly
Effects: Para. 3: discovered that Bill had many interesting stories; made the decision to travel by train
Para. 4: realized he was interested in working with the elderly; plans to focus studies on the elderly

 For additional practice with writing a cause/effect essay, have students visit *Q Online Practice*.

▶ *Reading and Writing 3, page 196*

Grammar: Complex sentences (10 minutes)

1. Read the information about complex sentences. Copy the first example on the board and underline *Beatrice was not very happy*. Point out to students that this part of sentence would be complete by itself if you put a period at the end of it. The second part is not complete because the word *when* makes it dependent.

2. Elicit sentences from students using the word *because* and write them on the board in two ways: 1) with the independent clause first and 2) with the dependent clause first. Ask students to identify the dependent clause. Ask which sentence needs a comma.

Skill Note

Because is less formal than *since*, and its use will be more familiar to students.

Putting the clause with *because* after the independent clause places more stress on the reason.

Since clauses are more likely to come at the beginning of the sentence and are often used when the cause is already known to the reader/listener: *Since you gave me that money, I've decided to go back to school.*

Students will probably be familiar with *since* as a time conjunction. (*I've known him since I was child.*) Be sure students understand that this is a different meaning for the same word.

Tip for Success (1 minute)

1. Read the tip aloud.

2. Elicit several sentences about the cause/effect essay in the previous section, e.g., *He brought lunch to the man because he had an assignment to help the elderly. When he started talking to Bill, he found out that Bill had an interesting life.*

A (10 minutes)

1. Ask students to work individually to underline the dependent clauses.

2. Read each sentence aloud and call on volunteers to identify the dependent clause. Ask a student to explain why sentences 2 and 3 need commas.

> **Activity A Answers, p. 196**
> **2.** Since there was very little rain all spring;
> **3.** When he invested $300 in the new company many years ago;
> **4.** because someone donated a school bus;
> **5.** since many volunteers came to help

B (10 minutes)

1. Ask students to work individually to combine the sentences.

2. Call on volunteers to read their sentences aloud. Tell them to say "comma" if they included one.

> **Activity B Answers, pp. 196–197**
> **2.** The village no longer floods since the villagers planted a hundred trees on the hillside.
> **3.** When the organization had received enough donations, it bought the new equipment.
> **4.** Mr. Kelly donated a great deal of money to the children's fund because he knew that the children needed a new school.
> **5.** Since people in the village suffered from extreme poverty, many families could not afford to send their children to school.

EXPANSION ACTIVITY: Chain Story (15 minutes)

1. Practice the grammar and prepare students for writing about causes and effects by having them write a chain story. Start them off with a sentence on the board: *Because someone donated books to the homeless children's program, Timmy learned to read. Since he learned to read...*Seat the students in small groups and tell them to copy the beginning of the story and then pass the paper around, with each person adding another sentence with *because, since,* or *when* to continue the story. Call time after the paper has gone around each group at least twice.

2. Ask a volunteer from each group to read their finished story for the class.

 For additional practice with complex sentences, have students visit *Q Online Practice*.

▶ *Reading and Writing 3, page 197*

Q Unit Assignment:
Write a cause/effect essay

Unit Question (5 minutes)

Refer students back to the ideas they discussed at the beginning of the unit about how a small amount of money can make a big difference. Tell them they can use the ideas to help them write their Unit Assignment essay. Cue students if necessary by asking specific questions about the content of the unit: *What effects did the goat have on Beatrice's life? What effects does giving have on the giver?*

Learning Outcome

1. Tie the Unit Assignment to the unit learning outcome. Say: *The outcome for this unit is to write a cause/effect essay showing how a little money can make a big difference. This Unit Assignment is also going to let you show your skill in using complex sentences, noun collocations, and the vocabulary from the unit.*

2. Explain that you are going to use a rubric similar to their Self-Assessment checklist on p. 200 to grade their Unit Assignment. You can also share a copy of the Unit Assignment Rubric (on p. 97 of this *Teacher's Handbook)* with the students.

▶ *Reading and Writing 3, page 198*

Critical Thinking Tip (5 minutes)

1. Have a student read the tip aloud. Explain: *We often have to participate in groups to complete activities in class.* Ask: *Why is it good to participate when you're working in a group? Why is it not good to avoid participating? How do you feel when someone in your group doesn't participate?*

2. Ask: *In your everyday life, when do you need to participate in a group? Remember, your family is a group, and your friends are a group. How do you feel when someone in a group doesn't participate?*

Plan and Write

Critical Q: Expansion Activity

Synthesize Ideas

To encourage active participation, follow up Activity A with a brainstorm mingle. After students have brainstormed with their groups, have them stand and quickly form a new group with two or three new partners. Tell them every student in the new group must talk about at least one idea they heard from their original group. After a couple of minutes, have them form another new group and repeat. Then have students return to their seats and add any new ideas to their notes. Point out that when they share and discuss ideas, they are synthesizing the information and putting it in their own words.

Brainstorm

A (15 minutes)

Ask students to work with a group to brainstorm situations where a small amount of money or an act of kindness can make a big difference. Display the posters they made at the beginning of the unit to help them come up with ideas.

Plan

B (15 minutes)

1. Direct students' attention to the graphic organizer. Ask them to choose one of the situations from Activity A and complete the graphic organizer with at least three effects.

2. Have students use information from the graphic organizer to complete their outlines. Elicit which part of the organizer goes into the introductory paragraph. Help students craft a thesis statement.

3. Elicit a sample topic sentence for one of the body paragraphs. Ask students to work individually to complete their outlines. Monitor and provide feedback.

▶ *Reading and Writing 3, page 199*

Write

C (15 minutes)

1. Read the writing directions aloud. Remind students that you are going to use a rubric similar to their Self-Assessment checklist on p. 200 to grade their Unit Assignment. If you have not done so already, go over the checklist with the class.

2. Ask students to work individually to write their essays.

Alternative Unit Assignments

Assign or have students choose one of these assignments to do instead of, or in addition to, the Unit Assignment.

1. Think of some ways that a small amount of money could help people in your area. What is the greatest need—food, housing, or clothing? What could you do to encourage people to donate to this cause? What effects would people see if they donated?

2. Prepare an advertisement encouraging people to donate to a charitable organization. In the ad, include some effects of giving to this organization—how it will affect the people being helped or how it will affect the person donating.

 For an additional Unit Assignment, have students visit *Q Online Practice*.

▶ *Reading and Writing 3, page 200*

Revise and Edit

Peer Review

A (15 minutes)

1. Pair students and direct them to read each other's work

2. Ask students to answer the questions and discuss them.

3. Give students suggestions for how to give helpful feedback: *You describe the situation clearly in the introduction, but your thesis statement doesn't include the effects.*

Rewrite

B (10 minutes)

Students should review their partners' answers from A and rewrite their paragraphs accordingly.

Edit

C (15 minutes)

1. Direct students to read and complete the Self-Assessment checklist. They should be prepared to hand in their work or discuss it in class.

2. Ask for a show of hands for how many students gave all or mostly *yes* answers.

3. Use the Unit Assignment Rubric on p. 97 in this *Teacher's Handbook* to score each student's assignment.

4. Alternatively, divide the class into large groups and have students read their paragraphs to their group. Pass out copies of the Unit Assignment Rubric and have students grade each other.

▶ *Reading and Writing 3, page 201*

Track Your Success (5 minutes)

1. Have students circle the words they have learned in this unit. Suggest that students go back through the unit to review any words they have forgotten.

2. Have students check the skills they have mastered. If students need more practice to feel confident about their proficiency in a skill, point out the page numbers and encourage them to review.

3. Read the Learning Outcome aloud. Ask students if they feel that they have met the outcome.

Unit Assignment Rubric

Student name: _____

Date: _____

Unit Assignment: *Write a cause/effect essay explaining how a small amount of money can make a big difference.*

20 points = Essay element was completely successful (at least 90% of the time).
15 points = Essay element was mostly successful (at least 70% of the time).
10 points = Essay element was partially successful (at least 50% of the time).
 0 points = Essay element was not successful.

Cause/Effect Essay	20 points	15 points	10 points	0 points
Student used a cause/effect essay to clearly explain how a small amount of money can make a difference.				
The paragraph includes vocabulary from the unit and collocations with nouns.				
Essay includes a thesis statement describing the effects of the situation and a concluding paragraph restating the main idea.				
Essay includes at least three body paragraphs describing effects.				
Student used complex sentences correctly.				

Total points: _____

Comments:

Unit QUESTION
Do people communicate better now than in the past?

Communication

READING • identifying the author's purpose, audience, and tone
VOCABULARY • using the dictionary
WRITING • writing an opinion essay with a counterargument
GRAMMAR • sentence fragments

LEARNING OUTCOME

Develop an essay about communication that states your personal opinion and gives a counterargument.

▶ *Reading and Writing 3, pages 202–203*

Preview the Unit

Learning Outcome

1. Ask for a volunteer to read the unit skills, then the unit learning outcome.

2. Explain: *This is what you are expected to be able to do by the unit's end. The learning outcome explains how you are going to be evaluated. With this outcome in mind, you should focus on learning these skills (Reading, Vocabulary, Writing, Grammar) that will support your goal of writing an essay about communication that includes your opinion and a counterargument. This can also help you act as mentors in the classroom to help the other students meet this outcome.*

A (15 minutes)

1. To get students thinking about the topic, discuss the many ways people communicate with each other: by talking on the phone, through email, though social networking sites, by texting, by instant messaging, etc. Discuss any methods of communication that seem outdated or are not used as much anymore.

2. Put students in pairs or small groups to discuss the first two questions.

3. Call on volunteers to share their ideas with the class. Ask follow-up questions, e.g., *Why do you text some people and not others? How often do you talk on the phone?*

4. Focus students' attention on the photo. Have a volunteer describe the photo to the class. Read the question aloud.

Activity A Answers, p. 203
Answers will vary. Possible answers:
1. I usually communicate with my family by using an Internet phone service. I usually text my friends.
2. I use social networking sites because I like to stay in touch with all of my old friends./I don't use social networking sites because I like my privacy.
3. She might be looking at a Web site or an email on the second phone.

B (20 minutes)

1. Introduce the Unit Question, *Do people communicate better now than in the past?* Ask related information questions or questions about personal experience to help students prepare for answering the more abstract unit question. *What kinds of messages do people usually send when they text? When they email? Why might you call someone on the phone instead of texting or emailing them?*

2. Give students a minute to silently consider their answers to the Unit Question. Say, *Let's consider traditional methods of communication, like phone calls, letters, and face-to-face communication. What are the advantages of these traditional methods? What are the disadvantages?*

3. Write *Traditional Communication* and *Modern Communication* at the top of two sheets of poster paper. Add subcategories of *advantages* and *disadvantages* to each paper.

4. Elicit students' ideas and write them on the poster paper. Post the ideas to refer to later in the unit.

Activity B Answers, p. 203
Answers will vary. Possible answers:
Lower-level answers: Email is fast and easy. Sending a letter takes a long time.
Mid-level answers: Calling or meeting people is better because people express themselves more on the phone and in person.
Higher-level answers: (Students may be able to describe examples.) Social networking sites let people communicate in ways that weren't possible before. I can send my friends and family pictures, videos, and links to articles very quickly, and I can invite them to come to events and join group conversations.

The Q Classroom (5 minutes)
CD 3, Track 5

1. Play The Q Classroom. Use the example from the audio to help students continue the conversation. Ask: *How did the students answer the question? Do you agree or disagree with their ideas? Why?*

2. Ask students to look over the ideas they came up with for Activity B. Give them time to add new ideas to their notes.

▶ *Reading and Writing 3, page 204*

C (5 minutes)

1. Ask students to look at the abbreviations and check the ones they know.

2. Elicit the answers and write them on the board. Ask students about other abbreviations they are familiar with.

Activity C Answers, p. 204
b. be right back;
c. by the way;
d. talk to you later;
e. got to go;
f. great;
g. just kidding

D (10 minutes)

1. Direct students to take the survey about when they think it's appropriate to text.

2. Have them discuss their answers with a partner. Call on volunteers to share their ideas with the class.

EXPANSION ACTIVITY:
Communication Discussion (5 minutes)

Continue the discussion about when to use various methods of communication. Write *phone call, email, letter, chat,* and *text* on the board. Then elicit the social networking sites that students use and list them separately. Ask students to discuss in which situations they use each method of communication. Write their ideas on the board. Tell students to note any information from the discussion that they think might help them write an essay about communication at the end of the unit.

▶ *Reading and Writing 3, page 205*

READING

READING 1: 2b or not 2b

VOCABULARY (15 minutes)

1. Direct students to work with a partner to read the sentences and use context clues to identify the definitions that best match the bold words.

2. Call on volunteers to share their answers. Answer any questions about meaning and provide or elicit additional examples of the words in context. Pronounce and have students repeat the words. Highlight the stressed syllable in each word.

3. Have the pairs read the sentences together.

> **MULTILEVEL OPTION**
>
> Group lower-level students and assist them with the task. Point out context clues and ask questions to help students connect to the vocabulary, e.g., *Do you know someone who is very **creative**? What do they like to make or do?*
>
> Have higher-level students complete the activity individually and then compare answers with a partner. Assign one of these words to each pair: *curiosity, restricted, consistency, creative, demands.* Ask them to look up the word family and write one sentence with each part of speech. Have volunteers write one or two of their sentences on the board.

Vocabulary Answers, p. 205
1. b; **2.** b; **3.** c; **4.** a; **5.** a; **6.** b; **7.** a; **8.** b

 For additional practice with the vocabulary, have students visit *Q Online Practice.*

PREVIEW READING 1 (5 minutes)

1. Ask students to read the introductory information. Discuss who Shakespeare was and when he lived (late 1500s to early 1600s). Make sure students understand the significance of the title. (In the play, Hamlet is saying, "Should I continue to live?" Shakespeare is a symbol of long-lasting language because his works are still read and performed today.)

2. Direct students to read the first paragraph of the article. Elicit their predictions about texting. Write some of the predictions on the board and tell students to look at them again after they've finished reading.

> **Preview Reading Answer, p. 206**
> Answers will vary. Possible answers:
> Yes, because it's convenient and popular./No, because every technology gets replaced eventually.

Reading 1 Background Note

Some experts have argued that literacy is improving among today's young people because methods of modern communication require students to be able to read and write, whereas in the past, a child could easily communicate in social situations without those skills. They also say that children have always been flexible in switching from informal to formal modes of communication, and part of modern literacy is the ability to switch modes when using different methods of communication. However, there is still concern that youth who don't have enough access to standard language, perhaps because of poverty or lack of schooling, will not learn how to communicate formally.

READ (20 minutes)

 CD 3, Track 6

1. Instruct students to read the article. Remind them to refer to the glossed words. Tell them to mark any unknown vocabulary but to continue reading. Ask them to set their pens down or look up when they finish.

2. When most students have finished reading, elicit and discuss their vocabulary questions.

3. Play the audio and ask students to read along silently.

MAIN IDEAS (10 minutes)

1. Ask students to read the statements and work individually to complete the activity. Tell them to underline the places in the article that validate their answers.

2. Call on volunteers for the answers. Elicit the corrections for the false sentences.

> **Main Ideas Answers, p. 208**
> **1.** T;
> **2.** F; not new
> **3.** T;
> **4.** F; the letters, symbols, and words run together, without spaces
> **5.** T;
> **6.** T;
> **7.** T

DETAILS (10 minutes)

1. Direct students to read the statements and order the details from 1–6. Encourage them to circle each piece of information in the article as they find it.

2. Elicit the answers from the class and write them on the board.

> **Details Answers, p. 208**
> **a.** 3;   **b.** 5;   **c.** 6;   **d.** 1;   **e.** 4;   **f.** 2

 For additional practice with reading comprehension, have students visit *Q Online Practice.*

WHAT DO YOU THINK? (20 minutes)

1. Ask students to read the questions and reflect on their answers.

2. Seat the students in small groups and assign roles: a group leader to make sure everyone contributes, a note-taker to record the group's ideas, a reporter to share the group's ideas with the class, and a timekeeper to watch the clock.

3. Give students five minutes to discuss the questions. Call time if conversations are winding down. Allow them an extra minute or two if necessary.

4. Call on each group's reporter to share ideas with the class.

5. Have each student choose one of the questions and write five to eight sentences in response.

6. Call on volunteers to share their responses with the class.

MULTILEVEL OPTION

Seat students in mixed-ability groups so that lower-level students can benefit from listening to higher-level students.

Allow lower-level students to write three sentences in response to the question they choose.

Ask higher-level students to write responses to more than one question.

What Do You Think? Answers, p. 209
Answers will vary. Possible answers:

1. I think texting has changed language. Some people even use text abbreviations when they're talking. I think texting is a bad thing. People are using incorrect language when they speak and write. If people continue to text, they will forget how to write correctly.

2. I agree with the author. Writing texts can take a long time, so texters have come up with an easy solution. Shorten the words! The author says there isn't consistency between texters. This means that each texter creates his or her own spellings for words, and I think that is very creative.

3. One advantage of texting is you can communicate quickly. Another advantage is you can communicate when it is convenient for you. You don't have to wait until the other person can have a conversation. Also, you can communicate with several people at once. One disadvantage is it's difficult to explain complicated ideas through texting. Also, people sometimes misunderstand texts because they can't hear the "speaker's" voice or see their body language.

Learning Outcome

Use the learning outcome to frame the purpose and relevance of Reading 1. Ask: *What did you learn from Reading 1 that will help you write an essay that includes your opinion about communication and a counterargument?* (Students learned some arguments in favor of texting that they may want to include in their essay. They also saw an example of how to integrate a counterargument into an opinion essay.)

Reading Skill: Identifying the author's purpose, audience, and tone (5 minutes)

1. Direct students to read the information about purpose, tone, and audience.

2. Check comprehension by asking questions: *What are some different purposes that authors write for? What are some examples of different tones? Why is the audience important?*

A (15 minutes)

1. Have students work with a partner to answer the questions.

2. Go over the answers with the class.

Reading Skill A Answers, p. 209
Answers will vary. Possible answers:

1. People who dislike texting. Because the author is defending texting and explaining the behavior of "texters."

2. to give an opinion; <u>all the popular beliefs about texting are wrong;</u>

3. serious/defensive; (checked in text):...texting has been condemned; It is not a disaster; ...[texters] know they need to be understood; Adults who condemn a "c u" in a young person's texting...; An extraordinary number of prophesies...linguistic evils unleashed by texting.

▶ *Reading and Writing 3, page 210*

Tip for Success (3 minutes)

1. Read the tip aloud.

2. Ask students what kinds of audiences they write for (e.g., teachers, friends, employers). Discuss the students' purposes for writing and the tone they use when they write for these different audiences.

21ST CENTURY SKILLS

The ability to comprehend texts requires more than just knowing the vocabulary and grammar. It's important that students are able to correctly identify the purpose, tone, and audience of texts they will read as employees, citizens, and consumers. Students will also need to be able to write texts with an appropriate purpose and tone for a particular audience. Ask students what kinds of texts they read or write in their daily lives or will need to read or write when they enter the workforce. Examples might include advertisements, inter-office email, news articles, letters, etc. Discuss the role that purpose, tone, and audience might play in interpreting or writing these texts. For example, distinguishing between texts that are written to inform and those written to persuade can require careful attention. Also, an email to a supervisor will have a different purpose and tone than a text message to a friend.

B (15 minutes)

1. Direct students to look at the examples of purpose and tone in the boxes. Then have them work with a partner to read each excerpt and choose an appropriate purpose and tone.

2. Call on volunteers for the answers. Elicit and discuss any differences of opinion.

> **Reading Skill B Answers, p. 210**
> **1.** to describe something, light and playful;
> **2.** to explain something, serious;
> **3.** to persuade the reader, serious;
> **4.** to describe something and entertain the reader, light and playful and funny

 For additional practice with identifying author's purpose, audience, and tone, have students visit *Q Online Practice.*

 Reading and Writing 3, page 211

READING 2: Social Networking Sites: Are They Changing Human Communication?

VOCABULARY (15 minutes)

1. Direct students to read the words and definitions in the box. Answer questions about meaning or provide examples of the words in context. Pronounce and have students repeat the words. Highlight the syllable in each word that receives primary stress.

2. Have students work with a partner to complete the sentences. Call on volunteers to read the completed sentences aloud. Help students identify context clues in each sentence that helped them choose the vocabulary word.

3. Provide or elicit additional sentences with the vocabulary, e.g., *Their voices are* **complementary**, *so it sounds nice when they sing together.*

> **Vocabulary Answers, pp. 211–212**
> **1.** debatable;   **2.** reconsider;   **3.** warn;   **4.** react;
> **5.** potentially;   **6.** shorten;   **7.** instantaneous;
> **8.** moderation;   **9.** complementary

 For additional practice with the vocabulary, have students visit *Q Online Practice.*

 Reading and Writing 3, page 212

PREVIEW READING 2 (5 minutes)

1. Elicit the names of social networking sites that students use or know about. Ask what they do on the sites.

2. Have students read the first sentence of each paragraph. Tell them to check their predictions.

3. Tell students they should review their predictions after reading.

> **Preview Reading 2 Answer, p. 212**
> (checked): Social networking sites might be dangerous.

Reading 2 Background Note

While researchers continue to debate the effects of social networking on the young, the use of social networking sites shows no signs of slowing down and is growing particularly quickly among people over 25 and women. Some experts predict that by 2014, over 65% of Internet users in the U.S. will be using a social network.

READD (20 minutes)

CD 3, Track 7

1. Instruct students to read the article and refer to the glossed word. Tell them to mark any unknown vocabulary but to continue reading. Ask them to set their pens down or look up when they've completed the article.

2. When most students have finished reading, elicit and discuss their vocabulary questions.

3. Play the audio and ask students to read along silently.

 Reading and Writing 3, page 214

MAIN IDEAS (10 minutes)

1. Ask students to read and complete the activity individually. Tell them to mark the place in the text where they find each idea.

2. Elicit the answers from the class and write them on the board.

> **Main Ideas Answers, p. 214**
> **a.** 4;   **b.** 3;   **c.** 5;   **d.** 6;   **e.** 1;   **f.** 2

DETAILS (10 minutes)

1. Direct students to read the statements and complete them with the phrases in the box.

2. Go over the answers with the class.

> **Details Answers, p. 214**
> **1.** a social networking site;
> **2.** real relationships with people;
> **3.** the development of illnesses;
> **4.** self-esteem;
> **5.** a lifeline

 For additional practice with reading comprehension, have students visit *Q Online Practice*.

 *Reading and Writing 3, page 215*
WHAT DO YOU THINK?

A (15 minutes)

1. Ask students to read the questions and reflect on their answers.

2. Seat the students in small groups and assign roles: a group leader to make sure everyone contributes, a note-taker to record the group's ideas, a reporter to share the group's ideas with the class, and a timekeeper to watch the clock.

3. Give students five minutes to discuss the questions. Call time if conversations are winding down. Allow them an extra minute or two if necessary.

4. Call on each group's reporter to share ideas with the class.

5. Have each student choose one of the questions and write five to eight sentences in response.

6. Call on volunteers to share their responses with the class.

> **Activity A Answers, p. 215**
> Answers will vary. Possible answers:
> **1.** I think people use social networking sites mainly to stay in touch with old friends. It's easy to keep in touch with a lot of people from your past on a social networking site. You can find out what they're all doing in a few minutes. You don't have to write or call all of them. I think people also use these sites to make plans with their friends and to share pictures and links that they think are interesting.

> **2.** No, I don't think we should be concerned about these warnings. I think that if people never get out of their houses and only communicate through social networking sites, they might have problems. But I don't think most people use social networking sites like that. The people that I know still see their friends and families even though they spend time on these sites. I think they communicate more now that they use social networking, so I think the sites are good for people to use.

> **3.** Yes, I agree with the author. I use a social networking site, and I do certain things with my friends online and certain things in person. My friends and I use the site to share photos and interesting things we find online. But we also use it to make plans to get together, or we use it to tell each other about events. Then we do get together and spend time face to face. If I didn't use a social networking site, I think I might see my friends less because I wouldn't always know what was going on.

B (5 minutes)

1. Tell the students that they should think about both Reading 1 and Reading 2 as they discuss the question in Activity B.

2. Ask students to read their sentences with a partner.

3. Call on pairs to share their responses with the class.

> **Activity B Answers, p. 215**
> Answers will vary. Possible answers:
> I think communication has been improved. We can communicate more quickly and with more people./I think communication has been harmed. People don't communicate long or complicated ideas any more.

Learning Outcome

Use the learning outcome to frame the purpose and relevance of Readings 1 and 2. Ask: *What did you learn from Readings 1 and 2 that will help you write about your opinion on communication and include a counterargument?* (Students read arguments in favor of texting and against social networking. They may want to incorporate some of these arguments into their essays.)

Vocabulary Skill: Using the dictionary
(5 minutes)

1. Direct students to read the information about prefixes. Answer any questions about meaning.

2. Check comprehension: *Which prefixes mean not? Which prefix means* again? *Which prefix means* before?

Skill Note

On the board, write some words with the prefixes listed on page 215. Have students guess at their meanings. For example: *bilingual; contract; defrost; incorrect, impatient, international; outsmart; preview, review, self-serve.*

Tip for Success (1 minute)

1. Read the tip aloud

2. Have students open their dictionaries, or class dictionaries, and find lists of common prefixes and suffixes.

▶ *Reading and Writing 3, page 216*

A (15 minutes)

1. Direct students to work individually to match each word with its definition. Encourage them to go back to Reading 1 to find the words in context.

2. Go over the answers with the class.

> **Activity A Answers, p. 216**
> **1.** d; **2.** g; **3.** a; **4.** b; **5.** h; **6.** e; **7.** c; **8.** f

B (15 minutes)

1. Have students close their dictionaries and work individually to match the words with their definitions. Tell them to check their dictionaries after they've made their guesses.

2. Call on volunteers for the answers. Ask students to find the context for the words in Reading 2. Have volunteers read the sentences aloud.

> **Activity B Answers, p. 216**
> **1.** d; **2.** a; **3.** c; **4.** b

 For additional practice with prefixes, have students visit *Q Online Practice.*

C (10 minutes)

1. Have students choose five words from Activities A and B and write a sentence using each word.

2. Have volunteers write their sentences on the board. Discuss the meaning of the words in the sentences.

> **Activity C Answers, p. 216**
> Answers will vary. Possible sentences:
> **1.** Some preteenagers have low self-esteem and little confidence.
> **2.** There was a lot of interaction between the soccer players on the field.
> **3.** I am unable to go to the concert because I have to work.
> **4.** Some people say that slang is nonstandard English.
> **5.** I dislike horror movies because I don't like to be scared.

▶ *Reading and Writing 3, page 217*

WRITING

Writing Skill: Writing an opinion essay with a counterargument (20 minutes)

1. Direct students to read the information about opinion essays.

2. Check comprehension: *What are the parts of an opinion essay? What information is in the introductory paragraph? What is a counterargument? What is in the body paragraphs? In the concluding paragraph?*

3. Ask students to look back at Reading 1 and identify the counterargument presented in the introductory paragraph. *(Ever since the arrival of printing, people have been arguing...consequences for language.)*

Tip for Success (3 minutes)

1. Read the tip aloud.

2. Elicit sentences using the arguments students have read regarding texting and social networking, e.g., *Some people say that texting is bad for literacy.*

A (5 minutes)

Direct students to read the opinion essay. Tell them to mark the writer's opinion and reasons as they read.

Culture note: If students are not familiar with the term "phone tag," explain to them that the name references a children's game played in many English speaking countries, called "tag." In this game, one child chases another and tries to touch, or tag, him or her. Once that child is "tagged," it's his or her turn to chase the others. In "phone tag," people chase and "tag" others when they try to call them and don't reach them, thus making it the other persons' turn to call.

▶ *Reading and Writing 3, page 218*

B (10 minutes)

1. Have students work individually to answer the questions and then share their answers with a partner.

2. Go over the answers with the class.

> **Activity B Answers, p. 218**
> **1.** (underlined): <u>This type of messaging is...fast, convenient, and fun.</u> (circled): Some people think that we communicate less frequently...on the phone.
> **2.** Reason 1: Typing messages is faster than using a phone. Reason 2: Leaving messages for people who can't respond right away is convenient. Reason 3: Using email can be a fun way to stay in touch with people.
> **3.** It's still important for us to hear the voice of people we care about.

 For additional practice with writing an opinion essay with a counterargument, have students visit *Q Online Practice*.

▶ *Reading and Writing 3, page 219*

Grammar: Sentence fragments (10 minutes)

1. Tell students that when you break something into pieces, each piece is called a *fragment*. A fragment is an incomplete piece of something. Explain what a sentence fragment is.

2. Direct students to read the information about sentence fragments. Elicit sentences with *when*, *since*, and *because*, which students studied in Unit 9. Ask students to identify the dependent and main clauses of the sentences and to explain the punctuation (i.e., that the sentence has a comma if the dependent clause comes first).

Skill Note

Because and *when* clauses are common sources of sentence fragments because we use them that way in speech: *Why weren't you here yesterday? Because I was sick.* Point out to students that this is just an example of standard written English being different from spoken English.

Also tell students to watch out for long dependent clauses. If the clause goes on too long, the writer may forget where he or she started. (e.g., *Although she used her phone for text messaging every day and almost never made any voice calls.*)

A (10 minutes)

1. Ask students to work with a partner to label each sentence *S* or *F* and to correct any fragment.

2. Call on volunteers to write the corrected sentences on the board.

> **Activity A Answers, p. 219**
> **1.** F, possible correction: When I can't talk to someone on the phone, I send them a message.
> **2.** S;
> **3.** F, possible correction: After I finish all of my homework, I chat with my friends online.
> **4.** S;
> **5.** F, possible correction: Although she's a very sociable person, she doesn't communicate online very much.

B (10 minutes)

1. Ask students to work individually to correct the fragments in the paragraph.

2. If possible, project the paragraph and have volunteers make the corrections. Otherwise have a single volunteer read out the entire paragraph, calling out the punctuation as he/she reads.

> **Activity B Answers, p. 219**
> When I was in high school, I was a very shy person. It was difficult for me to speak with people because I was so shy.
> Although I saw these people in school every day, there was something about talking to them on Bebo that seemed different.
> Now I have more friends than I ever had because I'm not shy on the computer.

> **MULTILEVEL OPTION**
>
> Allow lower-level students to work in pairs or small groups to complete this activity. Direct them to circle *when*, *because*, and *although* in the paragraph to focus their attention on the problem areas.

 For additional practice with sentence fragments, have students visit *Q Online Practice*.

Q Unit Assignment: Write an opinion essay with a counterargument

Unit Question (5 minutes)

Refer students back to the ideas they discussed at the beginning of the unit about whether people communicate better now than in the past. Tell them they can use the ideas to help them write their Unit Assignment essay. Cue students if necessary by asking specific questions about the content of the unit: *What were the arguments against texting and social networking? What were the arguments in favor of it?*

Learning Outcome

1. Tie the Unit Assignment to the unit learning outcome. Say: *The outcome for this unit is to write an essay about communication that states your personal opinion and gives a counterargument. This Unit Assignment is also going to let you show your skill in using vocabulary from the unit, words with prefixes, and complete sentences.*

2. Explain that you are going to use a rubric similar to their Self-Assessment checklist on p. 222 to grade their Unit Assignment. You can also share a copy of the Unit Assignment Rubric (on p. 108 of this *Teacher's Handbook)* with the students.

Critical Thinking Tip (5 minutes)

1. Have a student read the tip aloud. Explain: *We often have to defend our arguments, not just in class, but also in everyday situations. We can develop stronger arguments if we have good reasons for our opinions, and if we know what our opponents are going to say.*

2. Ask: *In your everyday life, when do you need to defend your arguments? Think of a situation in which you might have to do so. For example, what if you wanted to complain to a business about their service?*

Plan and Write

Critical Q: Expansion Activity

Evaluate Ideas

   Bring out the advantage/disadvantage posters the class created at the beginning of the unit. Have students contribute additional ideas that they read about or thought of during the course of the unit. Point out that they can only make their own arguments compelling by giving serious consideration to the arguments on the other side (i.e., by addressing rather than ignoring the counterarguments). They should evaluate their arguments and the counterarguments to determine whether they are valid or not.

Brainstorm

A (15 minutes)

1. Ask students to work with a group to brainstorm lists of ways people communicated in the past and the ways they communicate now, in the 21st century.

2. Call on volunteers to share their ideas with the class and put the lists on the board.

Plan

B (15 minutes)

1. Have students work individually to compare the two lists and decide whether communication has improved or not.

2. Read through the sections of the outline. Elicit a sample topic sentence for one of the body paragraphs.

3. Ask students to work individually to complete the outline. Monitor and assist as necessary.

▶ *Reading and Writing 3, page 221*

Write

C (15 minutes)

1. Read the writing directions aloud. Remind students that you are going to use a rubric similar to their Self-Assessment checklist on p. 222 to grade their Unit Assignment. If you have not done so previously, go over the checklist with the class.

2. Ask students to work individually to write their essays.

Alternative Unit Assignments

Assign or have students choose one of these assignments to do instead of, or in addition to, the Unit Assignment.

1. Write a five-paragraph essay in which you address the question, *Are social networking sites helpful or harmful to people?* Write an essay giving your opinion along with providing a counterargument.

2. Many schools have banned students from carrying cell phones. Write a five-paragraph essay expressing your opinion about this policy. Be sure to include a counterargument in your essay.

 For an additional Unit Assignment, have students visit *Q Online Practice*.

▶ *Reading and Writing 3, page 222*

Revise and Edit

Peer Review

A (15 minutes)

1. Pair students and direct them to read each other's work.

2. Ask students to answer the questions and discuss them.

3. Give students suggestions for how to give helpful feedback: *The thesis statement with your opinion is clear, but I don't see the counterargument in your introductory paragraph.*

Rewrite

B (10 minutes)

Students should review their partners' answers from A and rewrite their paragraphs accordingly.

Edit

C (15 minutes)

1. Direct students to read and complete the Self-Assessment checklist. They should be prepared to hand in their work or discuss it in class.

2. Ask for a show of hands for how many students gave all or mostly *yes* answers.

3. Use the Unit Assignment Rubric on p. 108 in this *Teacher's Handbook* to score each student's assignment.

4. Alternatively, divide the class into large groups and have students read their paragraphs to their group. Pass out copies of the Unit Assignment Rubric and have students grade each other.

▶ *Reading and Writing 3, page 223*

Track Your Success (5 minutes)

1. Have students circle the words they have learned in this unit. Suggest that students go back through the unit to review any words they have forgotten.

2. Have students check the skills they have mastered. If students need more practice to feel confident about their proficiency in a skill, point out the page numbers and encourage them to review.

3. Read the Learning Outcome aloud. Ask students if they feel that they have met the outcome.

Unit Assignment Rubric

Student name: _____

Date: _____

Unit Assignment: *Write an essay about communication that states your personal opinion and gives a counterargument.*

20 points = Essay element was completely successful (at least 90% of the time).
15 points = Essay element was mostly successful (at least 70% of the time).
10 points = Essay element was partially successful (at least 50% of the time).
 0 points = Essay element was not successful.

Opinion Essay	20 points	15 points	10 points	0 points
Student clearly stated a personal opinion and gave a valid counterargument.				
The essay includes vocabulary from the unit and words with prefixes.				
The essay includes an introductory paragraph with a counterargument and an appropriate concluding paragraph.				
The essay includes three body paragraphs explaining reasons for the writer's opinion.				
The essay does not contain sentence fragments, and the tone of the writing is appropriate for the audience.				

Total points: _____

Comments:

Welcome to the Q Testing Program

1. MINIMUM SYSTEM REQUIREMENTS[1]

1024 x 768 screen resolution displaying 32-bit color

Web browser[2]:
Windows®-requires Internet Explorer® 7 or above
Mac®-requires OS X v10.4 and Safari® 2.0 or above
Linux®-requires Mozilla® 1.7 or Firefox® 1.5.0.9 or above

To open and use the customizable tests you must have an application installed that will open and edit .doc files, such as Microsoft® Word® (97 or higher).

To view and print the Print-and-go Tests, you must have an application installed that will open and print .pdf files, such as Adobe® Acrobat® Reader (6.0 or higher).

2. RUNNING THE APPLICATION

Windows®/Mac®
- Ensure that no other applications are running.
- Insert the Q: Skills for Success Testing Program CD-ROM into your CD-ROM drive.
- Double click on the file "start.htm" to start.

Linux®
- Insert the Q: Skills for Success Testing Program CD-ROM into your CD-ROM drive.
- Mount the disk on to the desktop.
- Double click on the CD-ROM icon.
- Right click on the icon for the "start.htm" file and select to "open with Mozilla".

3. TECHNICAL SUPPORT

If you experience any problems with this CD-ROM, please check that your machine matches or exceeds the minimum system requirements in point 1 above and that you are following the steps outlined in point 2 above.

If this does not help, e-mail us with your query at: elt.cdsupport.uk@oup.com
Be sure to provide the following information:

- Operating system (e.g. Windows 2000, Service Pack 4)
- Application used to access content, and version number
- Amount of RAM
- Processor speed
- Description of error or problem
- Actions before error occurred
- Number of times the error has occurred
- Is the error repeatable?

---

[1] The Q Testing Program CD-ROM also plays its audio files in a conventional CD player.

[2] Note that when browsing the CD-ROM in your Web browser, you must have pop-up windows enabled in your Web browser settings.

The Q Testing Program

The disc on the inside back cover of this book contains both ready-made and customizable versions of **Reading and Writing** and **Listening and Speaking** tests. Each of the tests consists of multiple choice, fill-in-the-blanks/sentence completion, error correction, sentence reordering/sentence construction, and matching exercises.

Creating and Using Tests

1. Select "Reading and Writing Tests" or "Listening and Speaking Tests" from the main menu.

2. Select the appropriate unit test or cumulative test (placement, midterm, or final) from the left-hand column.

3. For ready-made tests, select a Print-and-go Test, Answer Key, and Audio Script (for Listening and Speaking tests).

4. To modify tests for your students, select a Customizable Test, Answer Key, and Audio Script (for Listening and Speaking tests). Save the file to your computer and edit the test using Microsoft Word or a compatible word processor.

5. For Listening and Speaking tests, use the audio tracks provided with the tests. **Audio files for the listening and speaking tests can also be played in a standard CD player.**

Reading and Writing Tests

Each test consists of 40 questions taken from the selected unit. The Reading and Writing Tests assess reading skills, vocabulary, vocabulary skills, grammar, and writing skills.

Listening and Speaking Tests

Each test consists of 40 questions taken from the selected unit. The Listening and Speaking Tests assess listening skills, vocabulary, vocabulary skills, grammar, pronunciation, and speaking skills.

Cumulative Tests

The placement tests for both Listening and Speaking and Reading and Writing consist of 50 questions. Each placement test places students in the correct level of Q: Introductory–5. **A printable User Guide to help you administer the placement test is included with the placement test files on the CD-ROM.**

The midterm tests for both Listening and Speaking and Reading and Writing consist of 25 questions covering Units 1–5 of the selected Level. The midterm Reading and Listening texts are new and not used in any other tests or student books.

The final tests for both Listening and Speaking and Reading and Writing consist of 25 questions covering Units 6–10 of the selected Level. The final Reading and Listening texts are new and not used in any other tests or student books.